S0-BAF-449

YEAR OF THE

OX

YEAR OF THE

OX

SEAN CHAN

STERLING ETHOS
New York

STERLING ETHOS
New York

An Imprint of Sterling Publishing Co., Inc.
122 Fifth Avenue
New York, NY 10011

ISBN 978-1-4549-4045-6
978-1-4549-4046-3 (e-book)

Distributed in Canada by Sterling Publishing Co., Inc.
c/o Canadian Manda Group, 664 Annette Street
Toronto, Ontario M6S 2C8, Canada
Distributed in the United Kingdom by GMC Distribution Services
Castle Place, 166 High Street, Lewes, East Sussex BN7 1XU, England
Distributed in Australia by NewSouth Books
University of New South Wales, Sydney, NSW 2052, Australia

For information about custom editions, special sales, and premium and corporate purchases, please contact Sterling Special Sales at 800-805-5489 or specialsales@sterlingpublishing.com.

Manufactured in Singapore

2 4 6 8 10 9 7 5 3 1

sterlingpublishing.com

Cover art by iStock/GettyImages: Alexaz_ (border), visualgo (ox); Shutterstock.com: simplyvectors (blessing symbol), sunlight77 (sign character)

Cover and endpapers designed by Igor Satanovsky and Elizabeth Mihaltse Lindy
Interior design by Christine Heun

CONTENTS

To my wife and biggest cheerleader, Emily,
for bringing love and laughter into my life.

To my friends,
for seeing me through thick and thin.

To my younger self,
who never gave up and told himself that
everything would eventually be worth it.

To my ex-bosses,
who thankfully did not promote me
because the stars had better plans for me.

AUTHOR'S NOTE

How It All Began

My journey as a Chinese metaphysics practitioner began when I was a teenager. My roots are in Taiwan, where the culture and practice of Chinese metaphysics remains relatively strong compared to other Southeast Asian countries. So it wasn't uncommon for my parents to have Chinese astrology books around the house. I was used to seeing them, and when I was eighteen, I finally picked one up and studied it in earnest. However, I never grew up wanting to be a professional astrologer or practitioner. Long story short, I had a really tough start to life. Growing up in a less-than-ideal family environment, I turned to astrology as a form of solace and a guide in place of my parents.

When I touched my first book on Chinese astrology, I approached the topic the way any other teenager would, flipping through the horoscope section in the newspaper. I wanted to find out what the day, week, and year had in store for me, and when my desires would be met. I never really gave astrology the respect and dignity it deserved until I was in my late twenties, when my life became particularly difficult.

I reached the lowest point in my life in 2012, when I was twenty-six years old. I wanted to find out why some of the things that happened to me had occurred, and I wanted to find a way to derive meaning from what I had been through. This time, instead of being satisfied with a superficial understanding of astrology, I went deep into its history and philosophy. I read whatever books on Chinese thought and culture I could get my hands on. I plowed through books like *I-Ching* and *Tao De Ching*, some of the oldest Chinese classics and the progenitors of Chinese thought and culture. Eventually, I got the answers I was looking for.

What had originally intrigued me about Chinese astrology eventually turned into a deep respect for what our ancestors passed down to us. I wanted to get into the minds of the ancient sages to find out what gave them the level of insight and wisdom necessary to develop these fascinating methods of forecasting someone's life. I had my own reservations and was skeptical of my own practice when I first started giving consultations, but time showed me just how relevant astrology still is in this day and age.

I am considered young to be in this field and had many skeptics when I first started my practice, but what kept me going was my desire to educate people so that this art can be used the way our ancestors intended, instead of being seen as some form of shortcut or magical solution to life's challenges. As more people become interested in astrology, more are likely to be harmed and misled, unfortunately, and I wanted to stop that. I hope this book introduces more readers to a deeper understanding of Chinese metaphysics and astrology. And if you'd like to read more, you can visit my blog at www.masterseanchan.com/blog for more of my views and information on how I debunk some of the myths and misconceptions in this field.

INTRODUCTION

What This Book Hopes to Achieve

With this book, I hope to present Chinese astrology in the way our ancestors intended. As you go deeper into the topic, you'll find that Chinese philosophy and Chinese astrology are inextricably linked. This book is not about forecasting your life, because that would not be possible even with your full birth details. Instead, this book is intended to let you take the first step into Chinese metaphysics and astrology by showing you what that entails and how you should approach it.

An Appreciation of Chinese History and Philosophy

The vast majority of books on Chinese astrology approach this topic in a tabloid-like manner, which provides a laundry list of vague descriptions on the zodiacs and the characteristics associated with them. The content of this book is not what you would traditionally read in books on astrology. This is the result of the courage it took to come out as a practitioner and declare that annual zodiac forecasts are hogwash—instead I hope to show how Chinese astrology is so much more than just your zodiac sign and that no one is defined just by the year they're born in.

I hope this book will help you gain a new appreciation of Chinese astrology, and that it changes the tone and can perhaps set a new standard in the industry.

Helping You Understand Exactly What the Twelve Zodiacs Are

Most of us, especially the Chinese, are introduced to the Chinese zodiac when we experience our first Chinese New Year. During Chinese New Year celebrations, we might have seen a practitioner in a Chinese traditional robe giving a forecast of the year for each zodiac and ranking them according to how lucky their year will be. And other people might have been told a story of how the Jade Emperor needed to choose guardians for the year and held a race, and the order in which the zodiacs occurred was determined by who crossed the finish line first. For most people, knowledge of Chinese astrology usually never goes beyond these two stories.

For practitioners of Chinese astrology, the zodiacs are simply astrological markers that ancient astronomers used to measure time. The order of the zodiac and the animals is nothing more than the representation of energies and the interaction of Yin and Yang, and it has little to do with the personality traits of a person. Accurately assessing someone's personality and forecasting someone's year requires several other pieces of information in a person's chart and the correct application of techniques. I hope this book gives you a glimpse into how that can be done.

Dispelling Myths and Misconceptions

This book aims to dispel some of the longest-standing myths and misconceptions about Chinese astrology and metaphysics, with the hope that people will begin to use this ancient art the right way or, at least, begin their self-learning journey in the right direction. This one book will not be able to condense five thousand years of Chinese history and all of the teachings and wisdom it has to offer, but I hope it will serve as a good starting point for you.

This book will make you question a lot of things—things you've read in other books and things you've read on the Internet. I hope it nudges you in the right direction and makes you wish to learn more and see Chinese astrology through the lens the Chinese ancestors intended for us.

How to Use This Book

The first part of this book will focus on laying the right foundation and introducing a brief history, as well as some theoretical concepts of, Chinese astrology. This will go a long way in helping you understand the history, development, and application of Chinese astrology. I would encourage you to spend some time beginning to understand the foundations of this field. It will go a long way in making sure you apply Chinese astrology correctly and will help you protect yourself from the malpractices of this field.

The second part of this book is probably the reason why you purchased it, as it has to do with your zodiac. I would highly recommend that you resist the urge to go straight to this section without reading the first one. The second part of this book serves as a general guideline on what to look out for in your chart. Although it is not meant to forecast your life, I hope it serves as a general guideline in explaining why certain aspects of your life are the way they are and also gives hints about what your chart needs in terms of the elements, which in turn will determine which years will be favorable for you. There are more than 7.5 billion (yes, with a "b") possible chart permutations and I would need to live several lifetimes to be able to finish a commentary on every single possible chart.

Why practitioners are able to decipher charts despite more than 7.5 billion possibilities is because this art of forecasting follows a strict law and pattern, and understanding the laws that govern Chinese metaphysics gives you the ability to decipher any chart that is presented to you.

PART 1

Welcome to the World of Chinese Astrology

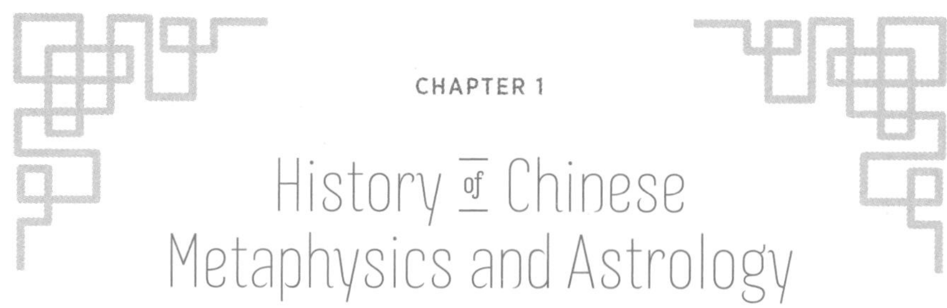

CHAPTER 1

History of Chinese Metaphysics and Astrology

The foundations of Chinese metaphysics and astrology date back to the beginning of the Chinese civilization around 2070 BCE, when *fu xi* (伏羲), a cultural hero in Chinese legend and mythology, first developed the Eight Trigrams, which represent the fundamental principles of reality.

Understanding the Philosophy Behind Chinese Astrology

To truly appreciate Chinese astrology, you must go into the minds of the sage and philosophers who developed this art. The theoretical building blocks of Chinese astrology existed from the dawn of Chinese civilization, even before the first dynasty of Xia. This was known as the Neolithic period—also known as the Sovereigns and Five Emperors—where several Chinese mythical figures were said to have existed. These mythical figures were said to have invented the tools and systems, including astrology, that helped the Chinese civilization flourish. You'll find that this is true for other civilizations as well, such as Vedic astrology from India known as *jtoyisha* and Western astrology, which was based on Ptolemy's work. Astrology was built from the calendar and then-current systems of timekeeping, so it's a natural by-product of those tools.

Although all forms of astrology share the principle of integration with the cosmos, there are certain worldviews that are unique to the Chinese:

The Cosmic Trinity

Called the *sancai* (三才) in Chinese, the Cosmic Trinity is a Chinese belief that everything is interconnected. This concept first appears in the *I-Ching* or *The Book of Change*, an ancient Chinese divination text and the oldest of the Chinese classics.

The Cosmic Trinity refers to the Forces of Heaven, Forces of Earth, and Forces of Man.

The Forces of Heaven are said to be predetermined and can be seen as our karma. The Forces of Earth represent our environment, which includes our family, people around us, and the surroundings in which we grew up. The Forces of Man refer to our free will and choices.

The Concept of Yin and Yang

The ancient Chinese had their own version of the Big Bang. Before the birth of Yin and Yang, there was a state of *taiji* (太极), or what some philosophers in the West would coin the Primal Beginning.

The ancient Chinese believed that for reality and its physical form to exist or manifest, there had to be duality or dichotomy. From this sprang the concept of Yin and Yang. Each and every phenomenon has a polar opposite. For every Yin, there is a Yang counterpart, and vice versa. The perceptive differences between Yin and Yang give birth to reality, but at the same time, Yin and Yang are also seen as an individual singularity, as one cannot exist without the other.

The ancient Chinese and modern-day practitioners view the world through the lens of Yin and Yang, as it permeates through all phenomena. From feeling the warmth of the sun and the cold from the absence of it, to the protons and electrons of an atom, and even to the formation of the two genders and different social classes in society—there is always an opposite phenomenon of whatever you can observe in nature.

The theory of Yin and Yang is a large part of Chinese metaphysics, and Chinese metaphysics itself is the study of how Yin and Yang's forces interact with each other. These interactions may be of a complementary nature, or they may be interdependent, or they can even be destructive.

The Five Elements: Metal, Wood, Water, Fire, and Earth

The Five Elements is a concept, or system, that the ancient Chinese used to explain the interaction between phenomena, from cosmic cycles to interaction between internal organs and even properties of medicinal drugs.

One of the biggest misconceptions in Chinese metaphysics is the belief that the Five Elements refer to the literal metal, wood, water, fire, and earth we can see and feel in real life. This couldn't be farther from the truth, and it's something that has not been clarified enough.

The Five Elements describe how Yin and Yang forces interact, and the concept has nothing to do with the literal thing each element describes. The theoretical way of describing the Five Elements would be:

* Metal - Yin energy at infancy
* Wood - Yang energy at infancy
* Water - Yin energy at maturity
* Fire - Yang energy at maturity
* Earth - Consolidation of Yang and Yin

Yin and Yang are always in a constant flux with periods of infancy, growth, strengthening, and weakening. The Five Elements represent this cycle (which is why we say that they are Old or Young).

The Five Elements are also used to describe the cycle of life and death:

* Wood symbolizes a period of growth and vitality.
* Fire symbolizes a period of rapid expansion and the peak of growth.
* Earth symbolizes a period when the consolidation of energies begins and is seen as a transitional period.
* Metal symbolizes a period when the consolidation comes to a halt and the rewards of our actions come to fruition.
* Water symbolizes a period of retreat and stagnation before we go back to a growth stage symbolized by Wood.

When you receive an astrological forecast using the Bazi method, you'll often hear that your astrological chart lacks a certain element. People sometimes mistakenly think that by incorporating the literal element they're lacking into their daily lives, their lives can change. This, again, is the wrong way of understanding Chinese metaphysics, and it's important we address this myth.

Let's take this example: The human body is fifty to sixty-five percent water. If someone's astrological chart does not welcome any more of the Water element, would that mean that this person is cursed with bad luck for the rest of his or her life, simply because physiologically they cannot be comprised of more water? Similarly, would someone who lacks the Earth element see their lives improve by coming into physical contact with or ingesting soil? No one's astrological chart is perfectly balanced, although some charts are more than others. Every chart will require a certain element to come into the picture to contribute or maintain that balance. This is what we call your beneficial or anchor element or *yong shen* (用神).

The bottom line is this: The Five Elements are a way of describing how energy moves, interacts, and unfolds.

Birth and Control Cycle of the Five Elements

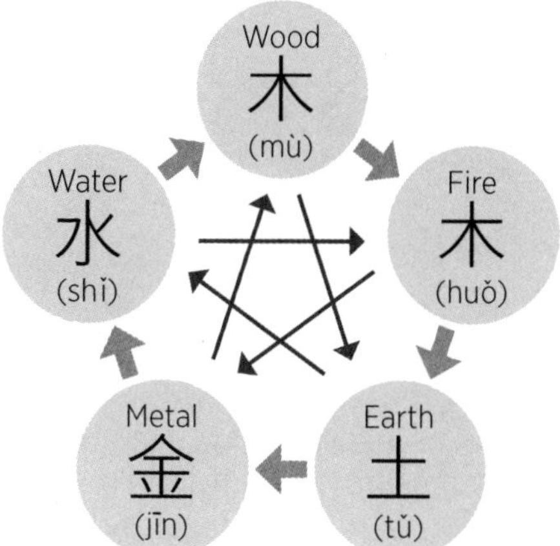

The above image shows the cycle of birth of the elements: Metal => Water => Wood => Fire => Earth and then back to Metal again, where the process repeats itself.

The thin arrows show which element controls which other element. You'll notice that the element being controlled is always the second one from the point of reference. Looking back at the cycle: Metal => Water => Wood => Fire => Earth:

* Fire controls Metal
* Earth controls Water
* Metal controls Wood
* Water controls Fire
* Wood controls Earth

Do not be tempted to associate "birth" with a positive connotation and "control" with a negative one. In Chinese metaphysical theory, birth is neither positive nor negative, and neither is the control of an element. What's important is the balance between the elements.

Different Forms of Chinese Astrology

Although the majority of people are unaware of it, there are actually several different systems of Chinese astrology.

Zi Wei Dou Shu: Polaris Star Astrology

Arguably the most advanced method of Chinese astrology, *Zi Wei Dou Shu* was the latest astrological forecasting method to appear in Chinese history and saw its developments begin during the Song dynasty (960 to 1279 CE). At this point, other systems of Chinese astrology were already considered mature or developed. Zi Wei Dou Shu became very popular in countries like Hong Kong and Taiwan and is still widely practiced. The Western name for this method of astrological forecasting is Purple Star Astrology because the *zi* in Zi Wei Dou Shu literally means the color purple. However, the more accurate way to interpret this phrase is to look at the word *zi wei,* which is a term used for the emperor.

Zi wei refers to the Polaris star or the North Star. The entire northern sky wheels around it, and this is the reason why the Polaris star is seen to represent the emperor. This school of astrology focuses on the position of the celestial stars and uses the Polaris star, the Ursa Major constellation, as well as stars from the Sagittarius constellation—and this is just the tip of the iceberg. Some of the stars used in this school of astrology are the same stars Western astrologers use.

Zi Wei Dou Shu arose during a later stage in Chinese history and is seen as more complex than Bazi, which we'll read about next. This is because Chinese knowledge of astronomy became even comprehensive as more scholars, and even mythical figures, began to develop on theories originated in earlier dynasties.

There are many stories surrounding the origin of Zi Wei Dou Shu. Legend says that this method of Chinese astrology was developed by one of the Eight Immortals in Chinese mythology, and some say it was developed by a gifted scholar.

Bazi: The Four Pillars of Destiny

This book will focus mainly on the Bazi method of Chinese astrology. Bazi literally translates to "eight characters." In the West, it's known as the Four Pillars of Destiny, as the astrological chart plotted under this method literally has four Pillars or columns in it. Each Pillar has two characters made up of a Heavenly Stem and an Earth Branch, making up the eight characters in one's Bazi astrological chart.

The theoretical foundations of the Four Pillars of Destiny method date back all the way to the Han period (202 BCE to 220 CE). It was already considered a developed method of Chinese astrology during the Song dynasty, when it first got its name. It was further developed and enhanced with each passing dynasty, with its theory and application reaching its peak in Ming (1368 to 1644 CE) and Qing (1644 to 1912 CE) dynasties, when there was a resurgence of interest in the Chinese metaphysical arts.

Instead of using the stars, which require a more thorough understanding of astronomy, an older method like Bazi measures the position of Earth around the sun using the Twenty-Four Solar Terms. The Twenty-Four Solar Terms represent the annual path or cycle of the sun, which served as an important guide for agricultural production in ancient China.

Which Astrological Method Does the Zodiac Belong to, and What Are They Exactly?

What astrological method does the zodiac belong to? The short answer is: All of them!

And, what are they? The fact is, the creation of the twelve zodiacs was not due to some race between twelve animals, as the story goes. This version of explaining the twelve zodiacs is a common way for parents to introduce Chinese history and culture to their children. For most children of Asian parents, this mythical contest was our first impression and understanding of the twelve zodiacs.

The twelve zodiacs are not themselves a form of Chinese astrology, but rather, a building block to understanding it. Let's talk about the real reason why the twelve zodiacs exist.

The modern-day layman commonly perceives the twelve zodiacs as an independent, arbitrary system that can be used to describe one's personality and fate, but in fact, it's part of an extremely complex system of timekeeping. Without the ability to track and measure time, astrology would not exist.

Timekeeping in feudal China, in the olden days, was done by tracking the movement of the planets. There was a time when people did not have clocks or man-made time zones. Being able to measure and track time was of utmost importance in order for human civilization to progress, so it's no surprise that every civilization had their own calendar system, and there are parallels across all of them.

To bring astrology into the picture: You may be aware that there are twelve horoscope signs in Western astrology, and it is no mere coincidence that the Chinese had twelve Chinese zodiac signs as well. Why twelve and not more or less?

Before people could measure and define how long a year took, they had to define how long a month, week, and day lasted as well, and all these were possible through astronomy. Working backward from the measurements of years first, the twelve signs we see in both Western and Eastern astrology are due to the planet Jupiter. Jupiter takes approximately twelve years to revolve around Earth, so this was our first reference point in the measurement of time.

Each of the twelve zodiacs represents the position of Jupiter during the twelve-year zodiac cycle.

Months were measured by looking at the Big Dipper's movement around the Polaris star, weeks were measured by looking at the lunar phases, and days were measured by how long it took for the sun to reach the highest point in the sky two consecutive times.

Our understanding of astronomy gave us the ability to measure time and create calendars. With the ability to measure time came the ability to observe patterns and the cyclical nature of all things—from its birth and growth to its eventual decline. This laid the foundation of Chinese astrology.

Is One Method of Astrology Better Than the Other?

Which is better, Zi Wei Dou Shu or Bazi? There is no "better" form of astrology per se. From a practitioner's perspective, choosing a particular method is a matter of preference, although each method does have its own unique strengths.

The Four Pillars of Destiny (Bazi) method is useful for giving a quick and accurate assessment of a person's life trajectory, their major milestones, and other turning points in their existence. Using the Bazi, an experienced practitioner would be able to gauge in a matter of minutes someone's potential for success and the areas in life in which they might experience conflict. This is possible because Bazi follows a very clearly stated formula and law. What Bazi does not do as well is go into the finer details of a person's life. Astrological methods such as Zi Wei Dou Shu are a lot more complex, so whereas an assessment can't be done as swiftly, this method does a much better job of deducing the root causes of the events someone will go through and the intricacies of cause and effect.

Each astrological method from every civilization is valid and legitimate, so technically, no astrological method should contradict another—they're not supposed to. As long as any astrological method is applied correctly, it will be able to give you valuable insights into your life. I had the fortune of getting my own astrological chart assessed by astrologers specializing in different forms of astrology, and my forecasts always led to similar conclusions that painted an accurate story of my life.

Common Misconceptions About Chinese Astrology and the Zodiacs

People love reading about their zodiac as a form of understanding themselves better, but little does everyone know that looking at your sign alone does not mean much in the grand scheme of things. The zodiacs should not be seen as a form of astrology in and of themselves, but rather as a building block of Chinese astrology.

Trying to interpret one's personality using one's zodiac sign is just one untruth in the world of Chinese astrology. Here are some other common misconceptions these days. Once you understand why they're incorrect, you can avoid misinterpreting or misapplying Chinese astrology.

Everything Is Predestined, and We Can't Change What's Written in the Charts

While it's true that certain things like your gender and who your parents are can't be changed, it is a mistake to think that astrology is predestination.

We have our charts read so that we can understand ourselves and the lessons we need to learn, and we use that information to make better decisions. Seeing astrology as predestination is a mental trap that should be avoided.

A few people can have the same astrological chart, but the place in which they were born, their physical environments, and their genetic makeup all play a role in how their lives unfold. Life itself is infinitely complex, and astrology has never presented itself to be the progenitor of life and the answer to everything.

Astrology is the study of certain laws that govern the universe, but these laws can be applied in different environments and do not take into account human free will.

Your Character and Personality Are Determined by Your Zodiac Sign

Looking at your zodiac sign alone tells you nothing about your character and personality. Not everyone born under the Tiger zodiac sign is a fierce, alpha go-getter; and not everyone under the Pig sign is slothful and spends his days eating and sleeping.

Practitioners of Chinese astrology will never, ever draw a conclusion just by looking at your zodiac alone. A proper analysis is a lot more complicated and involves several more steps, of which your zodiac sign is part, but not the core focus.

Annual Zodiac Forecasts Are Reliable and Give You an Idea of What to Look Out For

The charade of annual forecasts should make any genuine practitioner cringe. This is a practice that should be banned, in my opinion, as it perpetuates myths about Chinese astrology that lead people to make bad decisions.

From an astrological forecasting perspective, nothing constructive or of value can ever be derived just by looking at the zodiac sign alone. The Chinese scholars and sages who developed Chinese astrology did not intend for astrology to be used this way. An accurate forecast on how your year, or even life, will turn out will always involve more than just your zodiac sign. It requires your whole chart to be plotted out, which involves advanced techniques that annual zodiac forecasts will never cover. This book aims to help you understand the process behind a chart analysis, so that you may begin to explore Chinese astrology on your own and with the right footing. It will also help you get the most out of your next consultation with a qualified practitioner, if you choose to visit one.

You Cannot Be Friends or Partners with People of a Conflicting Zodiac Sign

You would have heard of certain zodiacs clashing with another sign, and that they are natural enemies. There are six pairs of clashes:

Rat 子 (*Zi*) ⇔ Horse 午 (*Wu*)
Ox 丑 (*Chou*) ⇔ Goat 未 (*Wei*)
Tiger 寅 (*Yin*) ⇔ Monkey 申 (*Shen*)
Rabbit 卯 (*Mao*) ⇔ Rooster 酉 (*You*)
Dragon 辰 (*Chen*) ⇔ Dog 戌 (*Xu*)
Snake 巳 (*Si*) ⇔ Pig 亥 (*Hai*)

The twelve zodiacs refer to the Twelve Earthly Branches we use in Chinese astrology. These clash relationships are a way of describing opposing energies of these Branches. The concept is similar to the major aspects in Western astrology: conjunction, sextile, square, trine, and opposition—of which "opposition" would be the parallel of a "clash" relationship in Chinese astrology.

There has always been a negative connotation to clashes, but in fact, they can actually be a good thing in Chinese astrology. Clashes represent change, and change can be positive, albeit tiring at times.

What this also means is that it's perfectly fine if you wish to marry or be in business partnerships with someone with a zodiac that is a so-called clash with yours. The way you approach life may be different, but that isn't necessarily a bad thing.

The Time on the Clock When You Were Born Is Your True Birth Time

This is a common error that even some practitioners make. The time on the clock means nothing when it comes to astrology. The method of timekeeping we use now, for example Greenwich Mean Time, is man-made and not a true reflection of the position of the methods used to construct a chart.

For example, the Four Pillars of Destiny method is based on the sun's movements or the solar calendar, so you should convert your birth time to solar time instead of the time on the clock. If you do not make this adjustment, there'll be a chance that you or the practitioner you approached would have plotted your astrological chart incorrectly, leading to an inaccurate reading. If you use the online calculator I refer to later on in this book, the birth time conversion will be done for you.

You Can Artificially Influence Your Astrological Chart by Wearing Certain Colors

You will often hear that someone's luck can be improved by strengthening a certain element that her chart lacks, and that this can be achieved by using colors. For example, if your astrological chart lacks Fire, you can make up for this by wearing red, or you can wear blue if your chart lacks Water. This myth is the unfortunate result of commercialization in the field of Chinese astrology. Life itself and the laws of the universe are not so simple that they can be influenced through the use of color. If colors and charms were a legitimate way of improving one's life, surely their effects would have been documented in books, but any real practitioner who has read through the Chinese classics will know there is no documentation of such practices.

The sages and authors of books on Chinese astrology have never once stated in writing that colors are a remedy, and they strongly advocated exercising free will, self-awareness, and the cultivation of the chart-holder's character. This is the only true way of transcending one's chart, because the study of astrology is, after all, also the study of cause and effect. If you can control the *cause*, you can definitely influence the end outcome. For example, if your chart shows that you're born with a quick temper, changing this side of yourself will definitely bring you opportunities that you would otherwise have been denied.

It is tempting to perceive Chinese metaphysics and astrology as quick fixes or magical panaceas for life's challenges. In reality, they were intended as more holistic ways to view your life and choices, against the backdrop of the universe. There is no reason for it to be conceived as something so reductive when it has so much more to teach us.

CHAPTER 2

Basic Concepts

In this section, I'll lay out the foundational theory of Chinese astrology behind the Four Pillars of Destiny method. Although you may wish to jump right into the analysis of an astrological chart to see what the future has in store for you, I would encourage you to resist that urge. Spend a bit of time trying to understand the foundations underlying your astrological chart, not just for the purpose of learning how to decipher it, but rather, so that you will know what to look for should you ever decide to go for a reading by a practitioner. Knowing a little about how things truly work will ensure that you get the most out of your consultation and self-study. If you aspire to become a practitioner, you will find, I hope, that this book nudges you in the right direction and helps you appreciate the wisdom that has been passed down to us.

The study of Chinese astrology is the study of nature's laws and its cyclical nature. To observe cycles, we need to be able to measure time. This section provides some background to the foundations of Chinese astrology and the lens through which the Chinese sages viewed the world.

The Beginning of Chinese Astrology

The first record of Chinese civilization was a Neolithic period known as the Three Sovereigns and Five Emperors. It's arguably the period that marked the beginning of Chinese astrology, as much of the theory behind it is said to have originated at this time. As I mentioned in the last section, timekeeping led to much of the theory underlying what we now know as Chinese astrology.

The very first system of timekeeping dates back to 2697 BCE, when the Yellow Emperor, one of the Five Emperors and mythical figures, ordered the development of a calendar. This was when the Ten Heavenly Stems were born.

The Ten Heavenly Stems

The Ten Heavenly Stems are a Chinese system of ordinals first used to measure time. Each Heavenly Stem had an astrological name to designate a particular position, but it has been simplified into the names below, which are more commonly used today:

甲 (*Jia*) - Yang Wood
乙 (*Yi*) - Yin Wood
丙 (*Bing*) - Yang Fire
丁 (*Ding*) - Yin Fire
戊 (*Wu*) - Yang Earth
己 (*Hi*) - Yin Earth
庚 (*Geng*) - Yang Metal
辛 (*Xin*) - Yin Metal
壬 (*Ren*) - Yang Water
癸 (*Gui*) - Yin Water

Each element has a Yin version and a Yang version. The Ten Heavenly Stems are made up of the Five Elements and their Yin and Yang polarities and they are used to symbolize the beginning and end of a particular period.

The reason why they are *Ten* Heavenly Stems is because, during this period, weeks consisted of ten days. Months were measured as three weeks, which made up thirty days. The days of the week were designated using these Ten Heavenly Stems. Despite the abolition of the lunisolar calendar in China in 1912, it is still used today for celebrating traditional holidays.

Chinese astronomy was still in its infant stages when the concept of the Ten Heavenly Stems first appeared. As dynasties came and went, the Chinese system of timekeeping was continually enhanced as the understanding of astronomy became deeper.

Just remember, almost everything you read in Chinese metaphysics has to do with timekeeping. The Ten Heavenly Stems represent a cycle, and each Heavenly Stem has a unique meaning representing an event, a person, or an aspect of your life. This information gives us hints as to what to expect from a certain year. Wood Stems generally represent new beginnings, Fire represents growth, Earth represents consolidation and stability, Metal represents change, and Water represents the flow of the change.

The Twelve Earthly Branches and the Jupiter Cycle

The Twelve Earthly Branches are the technical name for the zodiacs that track Jupiter's movement. Astrologers rarely use the names of the twelve zodiac animals when giving a reading.

If you're wondering why certain zodiac animals correspond to certain times of the day and certain years of the zodiac cycle, the animals are just symbols, an abstract representation of the energies these animals represent. For example, the Horse zodiac represents the 11am to 1pm segment of the day, the part of the day when it is hottest and Yang energy is most active. The same logic applies to other animal signs, so you'll find that the Pig and Rat zodiac represent the 9pm to 11pm and 11pm to 1am time segment, respectively, when the most Yin energy is present. Another reason why animal names had to be used was so that people in the past could better understand and apply this system of timekeeping.

Here's a breakdown of the animal signs and what they represent:

子 (*Zi*) - Yang Water. Rat. 11pm to 1am.
丑 (*Chou*) - Yin Earth. Ox. 1am to 3am.
寅 (*Yin*) - Yang Wood. Tiger. 3am to 5am.
卯 (*Mao*) - Yin Wood. Rabbit. 5am to 7am.
辰 (*Chen*) - Yang Earth. Dragon. 7am to 9am.
巳 (*Si*) - Yin Fire. Snake. 9am to 11am.
午 (*Wu*) - Yang Fire. Horse. 11am to 1pm.
未 (*Wei*) - Yin Earth. Goat. 1pm to 3pm.
申 (*Shen*) - Yang Metal. Monkey. 3pm to 5pm.
酉 (*You*) - Yin Metal. Rooster. 5pm to 7pm.
戌 (*Xu*) - Yang Earth. Dog. 7pm to 9pm.
亥 (*Hai*) - Yin Water. Pig. 9pm to 11pm.

The Twelve Earthly Branches serve a similar purpose as the Ten Heavenly Stems, acting as placeholders for the celestial sky and as a system of measuring time.

The Sexagenary Cycle: Bringing the Stems and Branches Together

Both the Ten Heavenly Stems and Twelve Earthly Branches have their own astrological origins and are considered two separate systems of timekeeping. Eventually, they were brought together to form a more comprehensive system to measure time even more accurately. Together, the Ten Heavenly Stems and Twelve Earthly Branches form the sexagenary cycle, which is the Chinese sixty-year calendar cycle.

Each year in the sixty-year sexagenary cycle is expressed by using one Heavenly Stem and one Earthly Branch, collectively called a Pillar in the context of one's astrological chart.

What Do These Have to Do with Your Zodiac?

You are probably aware of the fact that each zodiac has five corresponding elements. You could be a Fire Tiger or an Earth Tiger, or a Metal or Water Pig depending on the year you were born.

We will never be far away from the Ten Heavenly Stems and Twelve Earthly Branches whenever we talk about the zodiac, because the Twelve Earthly Branches *are* your zodiacs, and the Ten Heavenly Stems are what give each one its corresponding element. The sixty-year sexagenary is basically your twelve zodiacs and their five corresponding elements, and your zodiac simply tells us where we are in the sixty-year cycle.

For example, if you were born in 1974, the Heavenly Stem for that year is Yang Wood (甲) and the Branch would be *Yin* (寅), which represents the Tiger, making you a Wood Tiger. If you were born in 1977, you would be a Fire Snake, as the Heavenly Branch is Fire and Earthly Branch is *Si* (巳).

Understanding Your Chart

A reminder on ethics and responsibility: This section of the book is not meant to turn you into a practitioner or teach you how to forecast a person's life. It is meant to be a primer on how a chart analysis is done and what goes on in the practitioner's mind. It will help you understand the role your zodiac and Daymaster—the part of the chart that represents you—play when your chart is being interpreted and introduce the terms required for you to better understand your own chart.

As curious as you might be, please refrain from deciphering charts for others and attempting to forecast their lives. This should not be done until you are extremely confident in your analysis and have gathered enough experience to give accurate readings. Words, when spoken in the context of an astrological chart reading, can have a profound impact on someone. People are often in a vulnerable state when they go for an astrological reading, and if you're not qualified to decipher charts for others, you may end up causing harm or distress.

The Components of a Chart

There are a few components that make up a chart. These are the major ones you need to take note of:

YOUR NATAL CHART: This is determined by your birth date and time and is a reflection of who you are and the foundations of your existence. A natal chart consists of four Pillars: Year, Month, Day, and Hour. Each represents a certain aspect of your life. For example, your Year Pillar represents your parents and the family environment, whereas your Month Pillar represents your siblings.

YOUR DAYMASTER: This is represented by the Day Stem and is the part of the natal chart that represents you as an individual and your relationship with other Pillars of your natal chart. Your natal chart refers to all eight characters that appear, but your Daymaster refers only to the Day Stem.

YOUR ELEMENTAL PHASES: Your Elemental Phases can be seen as your life's trajectory, your macro-environment, and how you will develop as a person. There are two types of Elemental Phases: the Ten-Year Elemental Phase that changes every ten years, and the Annual Elemental Phase that changes every year. Everyone will go through the same Annual Elemental Phase determined by the sixty-year sexagenary cycle.

The minor parts of the chart are:

* Monthly phases
* Daily phases
* Hourly phases

These usually aren't looked into unless there is a very special reason or a very critical year in which you will need to pinpoint the exact month an event will occur.

The Natal Chart: Your Foundation and Starting Point

Hour Pillar (时柱)	Day Pillar (日柱)	Month Pillar (月柱)	Year Pillar (年柱)
丁 Yin Fire	癸 Yin Water (Daymaster)	庚 Yang Metal	辛 Yin Metal
巳 *si*,Snake	未 *wei*, Goat	寅 *yin*, Tiger	丑 *chou*, Ox

The above is a typical Bazi chart you would receive if you went to a practitioner for a reading. Your natal chart is basically a depiction of your birthday using the sexagenary cycle. There are four Pillars, with each Pillar made up of a Heavenly Stem and Earthly Branch—they are your Year, Month, Day, and Hour Pillars, which is why the English name for this method of astrological forecasting is the Four Pillars of Destiny.

Imagine this as a snapshot in time that shows where the planets were at the time of your birth. Note that when we refer to time, we are talking about solar time, which indicates where Earth is, relative to the sun. This is not the time on the clock representing man-made time zones like the Greenwich Mean Time zone that we use today. The time on the clock is not the correct time to use when plotting your astrological chart—adjustments have to be made by taking into account the difference between GMT and the time zone you were in at the time of birth, as well as the longitude of your birthplace. Do not worry if you don't know how to do this, as an experienced practitioner will usually do the adjustment for you. The adjustments made are usually not huge, so it might not even end up affecting your chart, because your Hour Pillar only changes every two hours. In the Bazi calculator I refer to later on, the conversion from GMT to solar time will be done automatically.

A natal chart can reveal things about you like your character, personality, family background, the quality of your marriage, and your overall capability and potential for wealth and success—just to list a few examples.

The Daymaster: The Part of the Natal Chart that Represents You

What practitioners usually pay attention to is the Day Stem, or what we call the Daymaster or *ri yuan* (日元), instead of your zodiac sign. The position of your Day Stem is indicated below:

The date shown above is February 4, 2021 10:10am					
时柱	Hour Pillar	丁	(Indirect Wealth)	巳	(Snake)
日柱	Day Pillar	癸	(Daymaster)	未	(Goat)
月柱	Month Pillar	庚	(Direct Resource)	寅	(Tiger)
年柱	Year Pillar	辛	(Indirect Resource)	丑	(Ox)

The other seven characters have different meanings and represent various aspects of your life and the people around you:

YEAR PILLAR: Grandparents. Governs the phase of your life from birth to 16 years.

MONTH PILLAR: Parents and siblings. Governs the phase of your life from when you're 17 to 32 years old.

DAY PILLAR: Yourself and your spouse. Governs your life from when you're 33 to 47 years old.

HOUR PILLAR: Children. Governs your life from 48 years old onward.

By analyzing the elements that appear in the different parts of the chart and the impact they have, practitioners can deduce the relationship between the chart-holder and his or her family, how smooth or tumultuous her life will be at each of the stages, and the way it will unfold.

Elemental Phases: Your Life Trajectory and What You Go Through

One part of the chart that laymen often do not take into account or do not even know the existence of is what I coin Elemental Phases, and the Chinese call 运 (*yun*).

People often like to use the words "luck" and "yun" interchangeably, but I wish to take this opportunity and say that this isn't an accurate way of conveying things. Luck suggests that events, especially positive ones, happen to us arbitrarily and for seemingly no reason—this isn't something the ancient sages believed in. The study of Chinese astrology is the study of cause and effect, as well as the laws governing the universe, and it has nothing to do with luck, per se.

A proper astrological reading cannot be done without looking into the Elemental Phases. Your natal chart, determined by your birthday, is like the foundation of your life and what you start off with, whereas your Elemental Phases describe the path you take from that foundation.

Let's take a deeper look into what the different Elemental Phases mean:

1. Ten-Year Elemental Phases (大运)

The Ten-Year Elemental Phases are a vital part of your chart that should never be ignored. They take precedence over the Annual Elemental Phases and hold more weight in determining the quality and auspiciousness of your chart, because they represent your macro-environment and long-term trajectory.

Traditionally, the Ten-Year Elemental Phases are considered more important than your natal chart too, because if there are flaws in your natal chart, you need your Ten-Year Elemental Phase to come in and remedy it. A positive Ten-Year Elemental Phase symbolizes the chart-holder being in a positive environment that helps in the chart-holder's growth and development. In other words, regardless of what your natal chart says, having positive Ten-Year Elemental Phases means that life is generally smoother with less obstacles.

2. Annual Elemental Phases (流年运)

The Annual Elemental Phases are the years we all go through. Everyone will go through the same Annual Elemental Phases in their charts, but our Ten-Year Elemental Phases will be different. For example, 2021 is the year of the Metal Ox (辛丑), so we will all have the influence of this Metal Ox in our charts. However, everyone will experience the year differently because our natal charts and Ten-Year Elemental Phases are different.

3. Monthly, Daily, and Hourly Phases

There is usually no need to go to the effort of looking into the monthly, daily, or even hourly phases unless there is a very special reason to do so. Practitioners usually do that only if the chart-holder is reaching a critical juncture, and the identifying of certain events is paramount to the chart-holder's well-being. For example, a practitioner can tell if the chart-holder is more prone to traffic accidents during a certain year, but the event usually has a higher possibility of occuring in a certain month and on a certain day. That's when going into the monthly and daily phases will matter. This logic can be applied to other areas too.

If a chart indicates that a particular year will be challenging, it would be wise to pay attention to the finer details in the chart throughout that year and even scrutinize charts from previous years leading up to a forecasted event. That will enable you to gather as much information as you can about the environment in which it will occur if you wish to stop it from manifesting. This is because the root cause of a negative event could be due to the actions and events from previous years, and assessing individual years arbitrarily without connecting them leaves out valuable information on how your life might unfold.

Not Just by Looking at the Zodiac Sign

We often like to associate people's dispositions according to their animal signs and what these animals are typically associated with. Dragons are associated with nobility and success; Tigers are associated with ferocity and ambition; Pigs are associated with sloth and a big appetite.

Your zodiac actually has very little to do with your character and personality. Not everyone born during the year of the Dragon will be extremely wealthy and successful. Similarly, not everyone born during the year of the Pig will be slothful and doomed to failure.

A deep analysis of your chart and the forecasting of your life require a practitioner to bring together all the aforementioned factors (and more), which can feel like an information overload for newcomers to Chinese astrology. It is never about just looking at the zodiac sign and describing someone based on the associated animal.

A Look at the Season in Which You Were Born

The Four Pillars of Destiny is a technique refined through the course of several dynasties, with different authors adding to the work of scholars from earlier dynasties. The Bazi method of forecasting was developed in the Song dynasty to the Ming dynasty, so that's almost one thousand years' worth of study and research.

One of the methods developed during the Song dynasty, it involves looking at the seasons in which a chart-holder was born, because the season of your birth has the largest influence on the strength of the elements in a chart. Charts can be categorized by whether it was too cold, hot, wet, or arid during a particular season, which would naturally affect the strength of each element in your chart.

Assessing the Ten-Year Elemental Phases

When a practitioner says your chart lacks a certain element, there is no way to artificially change that and make it appear. Neither is there a way to artificially strengthen an element in your chart. Hugging a tree or eating more vegetables when your chart lacks Wood or drinking more water when your chart lacks Water isn't going to do anything for your life from a metaphysical perspective. Remember, the Five Elements are a way of describing how energy moves. All charts are not perfectly balanced and have some flaws, and they will require an "anchor" element to come in to balance things and remedy these flaws. If that anchor element does not appear, it signifies an unfavorable period in your life when you'll need to make your decisions carefully to prevent any mishaps.

When your natal chart lacks a certain element and is in an imbalanced state, the only way to make up for it is to see if the required element shows up in your Elemental Phases. This means that the environment and your growth as a person are giving you something you were not born with. The Elemental Phases are an integral part of your chart and should always be part of any chart analysis. When the flaws of your natal chart are made up for by the Elemental Phases, it can manifest as you going through a period of meaningful growth, or it can be a reflection of entering a much better environment, or both. On the flip side, if you are undergoing a negative Elemental Phase, obstacles will likely manifest and personal growth will be lacking as well.

The Ten-Year Elemental Phases that appear in your chart follow a strict formula and can be seen as immutable. This is the part of the chart that the practitioner uses to forecast how your life would unfold according to nature's laws. That being said, whatever you see in your Elemental Phases will only come true if you are functioning on auto-pilot and lack self-awareness. The potential events in the Phases *can* be transcended, but that's a philosophical discussion for another time.

The Ten "Gods" in the Four Pillars of Destiny Method

The Ten "Gods" are actually your Ten Heavenly Stems. You might think having two terms that mean the same thing is somewhat redundant, but the Ten Gods offer us a way of describing how the Ten Heavenly Stems interact with each other using Yin and Yang and the Five Elements. Each of the Ten "Gods" can represent a multitude of things, ranging from your friends and family to a certain aspect of your life like career or marriage. The Ten "Gods" add another layer of analysis to a chart and allow you to see exactly how things manifest in different phases of your life.

To find out which Gods appear in your chart, you will need to know what your Daymaster is and its relation to the other elements appearing in your chart. You don't have to know the formula for how these "Gods" appear for now, as most chart plotters will do it for you. You can generate your chart here and see what your Daymaster is and the Gods, along with their associated Stems, that appear in your chart: www.masterseanchan.com/bazi-calculator. Refer to page 29 for a list of the Ten Heavenly Stems and their Chinese names for more insight.

Understanding the Ten Gods

My preference has always been to use the Chinese names of the Ten Gods during my consultations, but for the ease of everyone's understanding, we'll use the popular English names of the Ten Gods. There are five different categories of Gods with two in each category:

Officer Category

1. Direct Officer
2. Indirect Officer

Resource Category

1. Direct Resource
2. Indirect Resource

Peer Category

1. Companion
2. Rob Wealth

Output Category

1. Hurting Officer
2. Eating God

Wealth Category

1. Direct Wealth
2. Indirect Wealth

Each of the Ten Gods has a particular nature, as well:

THE POSITIVE GODS

The Gods that are usually regarded as auspicious are:

* Direct Officer
* Both Direct and Indirect Wealth
* Direct Resource
* Eating God

The above Gods are considered to have an inherently positive nature, but it does not mean that as long as one sees these Gods appearing in your chart, all is well and that wealth and abundance are guaranteed. Certain prerequisites need to be met in order for these Gods to show their positive side. These Gods do have their own negative sides too, but they are not as destructive as the Volatile Gods I'll be mentioning next.

THE NEGATIVE/VOLATILE GODS

The Gods that are considered negative are:

* Indirect Officer / Seven-Killings
* Hurting Officer
* Rob Wealth
* Indirect Resource

Before anyone jumps to conclusions, if you see these Gods in your chart, this doesn't mean that your chart is bad. A good life might have been measured by stability and minimal disruption in the ancient world when this system was developed, but these Gods welcome disruption and change, which might be why they were not highly regarded at the time. We can now understand that these Gods definitely have their positive sides, but, similar to their counterparts, certain conditions must be met in order for those helpful qualities to manifest.

The Ten Gods and Their Characteristics

This section elaborates a little on the five different categories of Gods that may appear in your chart and what they represent. We will not go into the formula for how the Ten Gods are determined, as a Bazi calculator will do that for you. However, this will give you some background if you see the term when you study your chart or if you get a professional forecast. Remember that these "Gods" are simply the Stems that appear, and whether they have a positive or negative impact on your chart depends on the overall balance of your natal chart.

OFFICER CATEGORY

People with an Officer God playing a positive role in their chart are known to have high titles or be in positions of power or influence. This does not necessarily need to be in the corporate world, as they can be thought leaders in their various fields too. They are often exceptional leaders with great managerial ability who often inspire confidence in others. An Officer God can also represent children in male charts.

When playing a negative role, Officer Gods will lead to the chart-holder being irresponsible, lacking a moral compass, and even experiencing ill health.

RESOURCE CATEGORY

The Resource God's symbol appeared on the imperial seal in ancient China. It represents scholastic pursuits and achievements, and also protection and influence. It represents the mother in both male and female charts, as the Resource God is always represented by the element that gives birth to one's Daymaster. The Resource God often likes to appear alongside the Officer God, as they form a virtuous birth cycle of elements that allows the chart-holder to tap into the positive side of both Gods.

When playing a negative role, Resource Gods cause the chart-holder to become lethargic and complacent. These chart-holders may also struggle academically.

PEER CATEGORY

The Gods in this category can represent peers and siblings. Chart-holders under the positive influence of a Peer God can experience considerable benefits through partnerships and collaboration. These people can be exceptional in the art of bringing people together.

When playing a negative role, Peer-category Gods manifest as chart-holders with a stubborn, self-centered nature. These people may also be in danger of losing wealth through others, for example through increased competition or by being cheated.

OUTPUT CATEGORY

The Gods in this category represent expression and creative output. When the Gods play a positive role in the chart, the chart-holder will possess an artistic flair and be very good at expressing himself or herself through music and art. He may also be an excellent communicator. As this is the God that gives birth to the wealth element, some chart-holders with Output Gods in their charts make exceptional businesspeople too. Output Gods can also represent a child in female charts.

When the Gods play a negative role, the chart-holder lacks the above positive traits and may instead be prone to overthinking and taking on more than they can handle. In severe cases, they will possess a rebellious streak and often get into trouble with authority.

WEALTH CATEGORY

The Wealth God represents a person's ability to acquire wealth through their skills and resourcefulness. When the Gods play a positive role in the chart, wealth will come smoothly and abundantly through the chart-holder's own efforts. It also represents the wife in a male chart.

When playing a negative role in the charts, it represents being burdened by wealth and the need to chase after riches, often at the expense of one's physical health or emotional well-being.

How Your Chart Is Analyzed

The ancient Chinese believed that everything valuable in nature can only exist when it is in a state of balance. The moment this state of balance is disturbed, harmony is lost and problems will arise.

For example: When Water and Earth come together in a state of balance, a lake is formed, and it acts as a nourisher of life. If Water overpowers Earth, the soil gets washed away and cannot hold water in place; when Earth overpowers Water, everything gets sucked dry and nothing useful or valuable is formed. The same logic can apply to other elements too. Two elements can bring out the best in each other, even if they oppose each other.

This theory is applied even to elements that have a birth relationship with each other. Using the example of Wood giving birth to Fire: Imagine throwing a huge pile of wood or logs onto a fire—you will end up suffocating it. Fire gives birth to Earth, but if Fire becomes too overwhelming, the Earth that is produced will end up being arid and compact and it will have no value, as it cannot be used to nourish life, such as crops. Although the word "birth" has positive connotations, in Chinese metaphysics, too much of it can be a bad thing.

If you flip through the Chinese classics on the Four Pillars of Destiny method written in the Ming and Qing dynasties, you'll often hear of charts being described by things you can observe in nature. An astrological chart that has too much Water will need Earth to come in and balance it, and also some Fire to come in to "warm up" the chart so that water can allow other forms of life to thrive.

Following this logic, a good chart is a balanced one. People born with balanced charts are deemed to have better lives, where things generally run more smoothly for them, and their environments are supportive of their growth. Imbalanced charts will lead to more tumultuous lives with constant challenges and unnecessary disruption.

Looking at the Season You Were Born In

Hour Pillar (时柱)	Day Pillar (日柱)	Month Pillar (月柱)	Year Pillar (年柱)
戊 wu, Yang Earth	辛 Yin Metal (Daymaster)	丙 Yang Fire	己 Yin Earth
子 zi, *Rat*	巳 *si*, Snake	子 zi, Rat	酉 you, Rooster

The season in which you were born is indicated by the Month Branch in your Bazi chart. Here's an example:

In the Chinese classic *Di Tian Sui* (滴天髓), special emphasis is given to the season in which a person was born, because it is the most important factor in determining the strength of the elements appearing in your chart. For example, if you were born during the season of spring, when Wood is dominant, any other Wood element appearing in your chart gets enhanced and strengthened. Its corresponding influence, negative or positive, will also increase in your chart. For example, if Wood is a beneficial element for you, being born during spring would be considered very auspicious, and this would be even more so if a Wood element appeared in one of your Stems as well. If a particular element is beneficial to your chart, you'll want it to appear in a strong manner so that it can withstand opposing elements and, at the same time, get rid of destructive elements.

Here are the seasons and their dominant elements:

* Spring: Wood is dominant. Earth is at its weakest.
* Summer: Fire is dominant. Metal is at its weakest.

* Autumn: Metal is dominant. Wood is at its weakest.
* Winter: Water is dominant. Fire is at its weakest.

Water is the weakest whenever it is an Earth month. There is no specific season for Earth, as it is seen as a transitional element that facilitates the process of change when the seasons change. Each season technically lasts three solar months, designated by the Twenty-Four Solar Terms, with two solar terms in each month. Earth months are also further split into Wet Earth and Dry Earth months, which will have different impacts on the chart.

The Five Elements and Associations with Human Virtues

The Five Elements are the building blocks of all phenomena, and this includes the values we hold as well. The Five Elements used in Chinese metaphysics were applied to Confucian philosophy, resulting in the Five Commons or 五常 (*wu chang*) being associated with the Five Elements we use in Chinese metaphysics. The Five Elements are often used in conjunction with the Ten Gods when deducing someone's character.

The common misconception most people have is that possessing an abundance of one particular Element means that you will exude the positive traits associated with that Element. This is not true. Having a chart full of Water does not make one intelligent or endow the person with high IQ. This goes back to the concept of balance. Everything that has some form of value or constructive use comes from a state of balance, and the best of a particular Element can only be brought out when balance is achieved.

Not having a particular element appear in your chart does not mean you lack a particular virtue either. What's most important is that the Elements within the chart are balanced, so that the best of the Element by which you are represented can be brought out. This virtue is your most outstanding trait as a person and the tool with which you can work toward success.

The Five Elements and Human Virtues	
Wood	Benevolence (仁)
Metal	Righteousness (义)
Fire	Etiquette (礼)
Water	Wisdom (智)
Earth	Trustworthiness (信)

Assessing Your Own Chart

Now the part you've been waiting for! The remainder of this book will be a general assessment of your chart based on the following, from two perspectives:

1. The zodiac you fall under and how the year of the Ox impacts you
2. Your Daymaster as someone under the Ox zodiac and what 2021 might mean for you

Please remember that a chart analysis encompasses way more than what is about to be covered, and this section is meant to be more of a guideline for you. To make the most out of the rest of the book, I'd recommend the following. Find out:

* Your zodiac sign and Daymaster. You can generate the chart at www.masterseanchan.com/bazi-calculator.
* The month and season in which you were born as indicated in your Bazi chart. These are measured using the solar terms and you will be guided on how to identify this on the calculator.

Your Daymaster and your zodiac element will be expressed using the Ten Heavenly Stems, whereas your zodiac sign itself and the month in which you were born will be expressed using the Twelve Earthly Branches.

Approach the next section with an open mind, and always remember that there is a whole lot more to Chinese astrology and metaphysics than what any author can possibly cram into a single book. This is meant to be a hint at the full scope of Chinese astrology—I hope that if it interests you, you will seek out more resources for further study.

CHAPTER 3

2021: The Year of the Metal Ox

In Chinese astrology and metaphysics, nothing ever holds its own intrinsic meaning, and everything exists as a duality. This is what the Yin and Yang symbol represents. Translated into laymen's terms, it simply means that everyone will experience 2021's Year of the Metal Ox differently. It is how we relate to it that matters. This section will explore what the year of the Metal Ox might mean for people under different zodiac signs and Daymasters.

The Year of the Metal Ox (辛丑)

When we speak of someone's zodiac sign, we are always referring to someone's Year Branch in their Bazi chart. The Twelve Branches and twelve zodiacs refer to the same thing, and each zodiac has a Branch that represents it. The Ox zodiac is represented by the Yin Earth Branch *Chou* (丑). Every zodiac will have a corresponding element. For our Ox friends, these are the elements you belong to:

* Wood Ox 乙丑 (1925, 1985)
* Fire Ox 丁丑 (1937, 1997)
* Earth Ox 己丑 (1949, 2009)
* Metal Ox 辛丑 (1961, 2021)
* Water Ox 癸丑 (1973, 2033)

This applies to all zodiacs: The element that your zodiac belongs to, which is determined by the Heavenly Stem that sits on top of the Branch, makes a lot of difference in how you will experience your year, because the elements your zodiac is related to will represent different things for different people. Traditionally, the Stems represent what the chart-holder receives from Heaven, and if that is something positive, it is important that this element remain unharmed. In theory, this cannot be changed, as the formula of your chart is fixed, so it can be said that a negative event is written in the stars. This is the reason why the Chinese sages preached self-awareness—it is seen as the only way to mitigate, or even prevent, the effects of these events.

The year in which you were born also changes how your chart is plotted, and that alone changes everything. It takes 60 to 180 years for the same chart to appear again.

The Ox Zodiac

First things first: Remember not to associate who you are as a person with the animals, or think that the animals have anything to do with your personality or character. They are just an abstract representation of the energies at a given point in time and a snapshot of astronomical positions. Not all people under the Ox zodiac will have boundless stamina or be hard workers or vegetarians (all stereotypical traits commonly associated with the Ox).

Secondly, in Chinese metaphysics, we can never assess the impact or meaning of any phenomenon when it is assessed on its own. Although each Stem, Branch, or zodiac sign technically symbolizes something, what it will ultimately mean to each and every one of us will still be different because how we relate to it is different. Such is the theory of Yin and Yang, because the Chinese sages believed that all reality exists as inseparable, but also contradictory opposites. They complement and contradict each other at the same time, and harmony is only achieved when Yin and Yang are balanced. As such, *Chou*, or the Ox zodiac, will mean different things to different people depending on whether *Chou* contributes or disrupts this balance.

To put Yin and Yang into perspective: The Branch *Chou*, on its own, represents the sprouting of something new because *Chou*, as an astronomical marker, symbolizes the end of winter. But what this exactly means for someone, as mentioned, still ultimately depends on other parts of that person's chart. For example, if you were born during winter months, then your sprouting process is hindered, because the birth of new things does not happen during winter. On the other hand, if you were born during spring or summer, then *Chou* takes on a different meaning, because growth, in astrological terms, is symbolized by spring and summer.

If *Chou* plays a positive role in someone's astrological chart, it can represent the chart-holder taking over a family business or continuing a family's legacy, because this Branch represents the growth of new things. It could also mean that the chart-holder's family will provide ample support to aid in the chart-holder's progress in life. As a negative example, some chart-holders might experience stagnation in their family instead, so that they are burdened by family problems rather than aided by family support. This is because those chart-holders can't get past the sprouting stage that the *Chou* Branch represents.

The only thing that a practitioner can tell accurately from your zodiac sign alone is your age. The real significance of what it means to be born under a zodiac still ultimately depends on what is in the rest of your chart, because the meaning changes as the seasons, and even days, change.

CHAPTER 4

2021's Year of the Metal Ox and What It Means to You

A lot of people often wonder what a given year's Pillar represents and what it holds for each one of us. On its own, it does give us some hints, but please remember you will always need to look back at your own natal chart in order to deduce what it means relative to you.

Everyone will experience 2021 differently, but whether you will experience its events as a positive or negative change very much depends on your natal chart and what part of the Ten-Year Elemental Phases you are currently going through.

The Pillar that represents 2021's year of the Ox is 辛丑, which is the thirty-eighth year of the sixty-year sexagenary cycle. Yin Metal (辛) sits on Wet Earth Branch of *Chou* (丑), which is the nurture (养) position of Yin Metal, meaning Yin Metal's strength is still in its infancy.

In Chinese astrology, the Heavenly Stem Yin Metal represents change, revolution, and new opportunities. Yin Metal on the Branch *Chou* 丑 does suggest a progenitive period of really big changes to come, with the forces behind those events starting to come into the picture. The culmination of events will probably be when Yin Metal is in its strongest state, which would be in 2028.

Traditionally, the Wood element is seen as the beginning of phenomena. Metal harms Wood, which is why Metal is used to symbolize change. The Yin

Metal of 2021 is a continuation of the Yang Metal which appeared in 2020, meaning the process of change has already been kickstarted in light of the 2020 pandemic. Again, how this impacts us as individuals really depends on our natal charts, and it is up to us to adapt to the events to come. Some of us will thrive because of this change, and some of us will not benefit as much. If your natal chart does not welcome Earth and Metal elements, then you'll likely find yourself on the negative side of these changes, and you'll need to take extra precautions, coupled with being proactive, to prepare for them.

Auxiliary Stars and the Zodiacs

You will always hear certain zodiacs being under the influence of certain stars every year. We call these stars "auxiliary stars." Each zodiac takes turns being under auspicious or inauspicious stars every year.

The maps of the stars and what they represent were already available long before the Four Pillars of Destiny method was developed, so it's only natural to see them applied when assessing someone's Bazi chart. The auxiliary stars that appear in a chart follow a strict formula determined by the Ten Heavenly Stems and Twelve Earthly Branches because, after all, they are astronomical markers.

Although the Four Pillars of Destiny primarily focus on the position of Earth around the sun, as well as the interaction between the Five Elements, Stems, and Branches, we do take the stars into account—although with a huge caveat.

Every Chinese New Year, you'll read that certain zodiacs are under the influence of certain stars in that given year, and that it plays a part in determining how their year will go. This is only half the picture. Traditionally, applying auxiliary stars is a secondary step, and the analysis using the Stems and Branches must come first. This is the reason why we refer to them as "auxiliary" stars—because they play a supportive role. It is the interaction of the Five Elements that dictates how a year will turn out for someone. The role of the auxiliary stars gives the elements their form. For example, if an auxiliary star represents a loss of wealth, this could manifest as the chart-holder losing money from a bad business decision, but it could also mean he spent a lot of money buying something that gave him pleasure. For example, the chart-holder bought a luxury watch as a reward or splurged on the renovation of his new house. Naturally, if you were this chart-holder, you would want the manifestation of this wealth loss to be because of this scenario. Whether manifestations take on a positive form or negative form will depend on the interaction of the elements.

If the Stem or Branch interactions are positive, the effects of positive auxiliary stars associated with that particular Stem or Branch will be amplified, and the effects of the negative auxiliary stars will be negligible, or vice versa. So, the next time you see your zodiac sign under the influence of a star representing sickness or trouble with authority, don't jump to conclusions, because it may not apply to you or it might be something totally insignificant. Relax.

Relationship Between the Twelve Zodiacs Using Branches

The Year Pillar in your astrological chart holds special significance because it represents your *taisui*, or what is commonly known as the Grand Duke, which governs the energies or events of a particular year. While the Grand Duke can represent parents and superiors, it also governs how smooth things will be on an environmental and macro level and basically tells us whether the Heavens will be on our side. In other words, the Year Pillar will be the one that will determine whether you can look back and tell yourself "the year went well," instead of only being able to say, "I had a few good months, or weeks, this year."

The zodiac signs, represented by the Branches, have special relationships and interactions with each other that result in the strengthening or weakening of elements. Each new year represents a different zodiac, or Branch, and it brings along a different interaction with the Year Pillar on your chart.

The differences and nuances come from how this is done, and exactly how each element is impacted. For example, the influence and impact on a particular element can be direct or indirect. An element can be weakened directly in the form of a clash, or indirectly by removing an element that supports it. All these interactions will manifest differently in real life.

You will often hear of terms like:

* Clash (冲): Involves two opposing elements, which may lead to the displacement, removal, and, sometimes, the strengthening of an element.
* Harmony (合): Describes the birth process of an element.
* Punishment (刑): Describes the process of certain elements being harmed during the birth process of another.
* Break (破): Occurs when an element overpowers another element.
* Harm (害): Indirectly weakens another element by preventing its strengthening.

Do not be misled by these terms, as none of them is intrinsically positive or negative. The terms used are merely a description of how the Branches interact with each other and the effect on the elements associated with each one. A clash might sound negative, but it actually represents change, and change can be good sometimes. The same goes for punishment, break, and harm—as negative as they sound, there are occasions when these interactions are positive, although the process often manifests along with some discomfort for the chart-holder. Similarly, although the word "harmony" has positive connotations, it can represent unwanted attachments or burdens, so the real meaning behind the word 合 (*he*) is often misinterpreted and lost in translation.

Again, the correct way to approach Chinese astrology is to know that there are always two sides to the same coin. As you approach Chinese astrology and get introduced to the basics, *always* remember that nothing in nature is intrinsically good or bad, and the bottom line is always about balance.

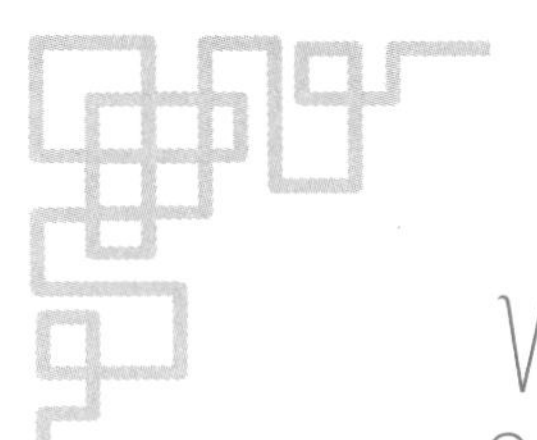

CHAPTER 5

What Each Zodiac Can Expect in 2021

A practitioner will not be able to forecast the year accurately for you unless your whole astrological chart is deciphered. Your zodiac sign is less than one-eighth of the information we need.

This section will not break down each zodiac by its corresponding element, as breaking it down at this point will be meaningless unless the whole chart is assessed. Here is a tip to get around this, though: As 2021 is represented by the Pillar 辛丑, which is Yin Metal sitting on a Yin Earth Branch, the impact on you will very much depend on the role Earth, Metal, and the *Chou* Branch play in your chart, and whether they push your chart toward balance or disrupt it instead. Regardless of which element your zodiac falls under, you always have to fall back on the roles Earth and Metal play in your chart.

The next section presents all twelve zodiacs and their relationship to the Ox zodiac, as well as the auxiliary stars that will influence each zodiac sign in 2021. Before we begin, once again, remember that an accurate and meaningful forecast can only be done if a practitioner has your full birth chart. A single change in the chart changes everything. A change in your Daymaster changes the Gods that appear in your chart, and every God has a different meaning. A change in any Stem or Branch alters the state of the chart, and the strength of the elements due to the different interactions between them. For example, for a Wood Daymaster person, Earth will represent wealth and the father, but for a Metal Daymaster person, Earth will represent protection and the mother. Therefore, every single person under the same zodiac sign will experience the year differently.

Even if you find two people with the exact same chart, how events manifest will still differ due to the era, birthplace, and general environment the chart-holder is born into, although there will be similarities. For example, if a banker and farmer had similar charts, the banker may experience job loss while the farmer experiences a bad harvest. Their overall picture and story will be the same, but the exact manifestation is different. If you ever have the fortune of meeting someone with the exact same chart as you, you'll get what I mean.

Do not—I repeat, do not—see this section as a full, detailed forecast of your year, because that is simply impossible without your full chart, and I don't want anyone to panic or become overly optimistic for nothing. Instead, try to see these forecasts as guidelines for what might happen in your year, and an example of how people under the same zodiac can experience the years differently, as well as how the auxiliary stars can play a part in how events unfold. Each zodiac will be presented with both a positive and negative manifestation of these features so that you can have a sense of the range of outcomes.

Rat (Zi 子)

For people under the Rat zodiac, the Branches of *Zi* and *Chou* have a relationship with each other called 六合 (*liu he*), which is called a six-harmony combination in English. The Earth element strengthens and Water element weakens in this relationship, but how this will manifest in real life depends on what your Daymaster is and the relationship the Earth and Water elements have with it. People under the Rat zodiac will be under the influence of an auxiliary star related to scholastic pursuits we call 文昌 (*wen chang*) and minor health ailments we call 病符 (*bing fu*).

POSITIVE MANIFESTATIONS: A six-harmony relationship suggests no major changes in your life this year; changes are usually represented by a clash. If the strengthening of Earth and weakening of Water is a positive sign for your chart, it symbolizes receiving help from benefactors or peers. The kind of help you receive will be behind the scenes, and you might not even know it's happening. The year 2021 will be an extremely good time to further your studies or learn something new.

NEGATIVE MANIFESTATIONS: If the six-harmony relationship between the Ox and Rat turns out to be a negative one, the obstacles will manifest as unwanted burdens and partnerships, or perhaps a recurring health issue that comes back to bother you. If you find this to be true, it's time to reconsider who you are working with, and it's also time to look after your health. Note that partnerships do not refer to romantic relationships and marriages; the Year Pillar does not govern relationships.

Ox (Chou 丑)

From a theoretical perspective, when you encounter your own zodiac year, the effects of the element it represents are amplified. In this case, the strength of Earth is amplified, and how the year will go for you as someone under the Ox zodiac will depend on the role Earth plays. Expect positives to feel even more positive, but the reverse will be the same too. Oxen are under the influence of auxiliary stars representing progress (岁驾 *sui jia*), arts and religion (华盖 *hua gai*), and major health issues (伏尸 *fu shi*).

POSITIVE MANIFESTATIONS: If the Earth element serves as a positive element in your chart, it is likely that Metal will be a positive element too. Given the auspicious auxiliary stars that appear, whatever you've been working on will come to fruition and you'll be reaping the rewards this year. As the Year Branch of *Chou* represents the new beginnings, you can also expect a new project or endeavor to go well. Don't be afraid to pursue a new hobby or area of interest as 华盖 (*hua gai*) appears this year.

NEGATIVE MANIFESTATIONS: When *Chou* plays a negative role in your chart, you might find that things don't move past new beginnings and lead to growth. You'll find it hard to complete things you've set out to do, and past projects you've been working on will likely fall through the cracks. The year 2021 will likely be one of stagnation and lethargy, so it's important that you remind yourself to be proactive instead of going with the flow. For the minority, depending on how your chart is structured, your health will likely take a hit due to the 伏尸 (*fu shi*) star.

Tiger (Yin 寅)

The Yin Wood Branch marks the start of spring and comes right after *Chou*. It marks the official start of growth in the cycle of the Twelve Earthly Branches. People under the Tiger zodiac are considered blessed in 2021, as auspicious auxiliary stars such as 天乙 (*tian yi*) land in the *Yin* Branch this year, so expect to receive a lot of help regardless of your situation.

POSITIVE MANIFESTATIONS: Earth represents Wood's wealth, because Wood needs to root itself into Earth in order to grow. The year 2021's elements act as a source of nourishment for people under the Tiger zodiac and, coupled with the auspicious auxiliary star of *tian yi*, people experiencing a positive year can expect opportunities related to wealth and career, as well as a lot of help from benefactors in unexpected places.

NEGATIVE MANIFESTATIONS: As the *Yin* and *Chou* Branches do not have any special interactions with each other, a relatively calm year can be expected, and major changes aren't expected. However, it will be a physically and emotionally exhausting year if the Earth element plays a negative role in your chart. Auxiliary stars representing solitude land in the *Yin* Branch, so your emotional well-being will take a slight toll—make sure you head out and socialize. It's one of those years when reminding yourself about work–life balance is important.

Rabbit (Mao 卯)

The Branch representing the Rabbit does not have any special interactions with the Branch representing the Ox, so like our Tiger friends, a relatively calm year is to be expected. Rabbits will be under the influence of a few negative auxiliary stars that affect parents' health (丧门 *sang men*) and their own emotional well-being (披头 *pi tou*), but please remember that this will not apply to everyone. Whether the influences of these stars manifest will depend on your whole chart.

POSITIVE MANIFESTATIONS: Small achievements are attainable. As people under the Rabbit zodiac are not under the influence of positive auxiliary stars this year, they'll likely need to rely on themselves, as opportunities won't present themselves so easily. It will be a peaceful year for Rabbits, provided that the Earth element isn't disrupting the balance of their charts.

NEGATIVE MANIFESTATIONS: Note that this scenario will not apply to everyone under the Rabbit zodiac but rather only to those whose charts show Earth and Metal elements posing a major disruption to their charts' balance. As negative auxiliary stars representing sickness of parents appear in the Year Pillar, a minority of Rabbits will need to pay close attention to their parents' health. Others might spread themselves too thin emotionally, so make sure you take some time for self-care when needed.

Dragon (Chen 辰)

Although the *Chen* Branch is made up of Earth too, the *Chou* Branch has a break relationship with it. All Earth Branches have Hidden Elements, because Earth Branches represent transition periods, and the breaking happens when the Hidden Elements clash with each other. Dragons are expected to have a slightly tougher year because of these clashes, which will likely involve both positive and destructive elements in their charts. Dragons will be under the influence of negative auxiliary stars representing conflict (贯索 *guan suo*) and estrangement (勾神 *gou shen*).

POSITIVE MANIFESTATIONS: A minority of people under the Dragon zodiac can still experience positive manifestations during the year 2021, although even those scenarios will likely involve some unpleasantness and an uphill climb, because it's very likely that both one's positive and destructive elements will be harmed as a result of the Branch interactions, so manifestations of these charts in daily life will be a mix of good and bad. Whether you're able to overcome these difficulties easily will depend on whether your positive elements are supported.

NEGATIVE MANIFESTATIONS: If the clash of the elements leads to your destructive elements strengthening and positive ones weakening, expect a conflict-prone year filled with obstacles. The consolation is that you'll be under the influence of an auxiliary star representing female benefactors, so some help can be expected.

Snake (Si 巳)

The Branch representing the Snake has a three-harmony relationship with the Branch representing the Ox, which leads to the strengthening of Metal. People under the Snake zodiac are blessed by positive auspicious stars like 国印 (*guo yin*) and 天德 (*tian de*), representing title and benefactors, respectively. People with Earth and Metal elements acting as their beneficial elements will benefit a lot from these stars.

POSITIVE MANIFESTATIONS: If you're one of the lucky ones with a chart in which Earth and Metal play a positive role, you can expect an extremely good year when you'll receive recognition. At work, a promotion is very likely. Wealth, naturally, will follow.

NEGATIVE MANIFESTATIONS: Remember—not every person under the Snake zodiac will receive a promotion, as the auxiliary stars should be considered only after the other elements in your chart are analyzed. If the Earth and Metal elements play destructive roles in your chart, you might just end up getting more responsibilities but without the benefits, so remember to negotiate, and don't sell yourself short.

Horse (Wu 午)

The *Wu* Branch representing the Horse is of the Fire element and has a harm relationship with the *Chou* Branch representing the Ox. Fire harms the Water and Metal hidden inside the *Chou* Branch, while Wet Earth *Chou* weakens Fire. This combination indicates a beneficial relationship turning sour. People under the Horse zodiac will have auxiliary stars representing minor wealth loss (小耗 *xiao hao*), and health ailments (死符 *si fu*) will also influence them.

POSITIVE MANIFESTATIONS: Despite the negative relationship the Horse and Ox share, people under the Horse zodiac still stand a chance of having a positive year if the Earth and Metal elements are positive forces in their charts. In that case, a higher title or promotion is to be expected. The caveat here would be to ensure that this is not taken for granted in case things change. Don't celebrate that promotion until it is officially yours as the Branch interactions do hold certain negative connotations such as poorer people relationships.

NEGATIVE MANIFESTATIONS: The harm relationship that the Ox and Horse share with each other usually denotes souring relationships, so expect this to be a major feature of the year. Given that Horses are under the influence of auxiliary stars representing minor wealth loss, expect relationships to sour due to money issues. Chart-holders who have Earth or Metal as their destructive elements will not experience progress in the career and wealth department, either.

Goat (Wei 未)

People under the Goat zodiac are in for a year of change, because the Goat and Ox have a clash relationship with each other. Changes always feel tiring, but whether the change is worth it and has a good ending heavily depends on whether your chart needs Earth and Metal. The Goat zodiac will be under the influence of an auxiliary star representing major wealth loss (大耗 *da hao*).

POSITIVE MANIFESTATIONS: Do not be afraid just because your zodiac has a clash relationship with the presiding year's zodiac. Clashes in zodiacs represent change, but change can be good, albeit tiring. Should a clash between the Goat and Ox be a positive sign in your chart, you might end up in a different job, or issues that have not been dealt with in years past will resolve themselves. The year will feel like a negative year because it'll be tiring, but you'll soon be able to look back and appreciate the positive significance of 2021.

NEGATIVE MANIFESTATIONS: The clash between Horse and Ox strengthens the Earth element, and the presence of Yin Metal produces Water and harms Wood. Anyone with Earth or Metal as their destructive elements or Wood as their positive element will be faced with a challenging year with negative changes forced upon them. As the auxiliary star representing major wealth loss is present, you might lose your job this year, and investments are unlikely to go well. Trying to maintain stability and the status quo should be a priority.

Monkey (Shen 申)

The Branches representing the Ox and Monkey zodiacs do not have any special interactions with each other. As the Monkey zodiac is represented by Metal, which Earth, represented by Ox, supports, most people under this zodiac are expected to have relatively peaceful year—unless their charts are severely imbalanced. This zodiac is under the blessing of auspicious auxiliary stars representing position and power (紫微 *zi wei*) and celebrations (天喜 *tian xi*) but are also under the influence of negative stars representing deceit (亡神 *wang shen*) and punishment (天厄 *tian e*).

POSITIVE MANIFESTATIONS: For Monkeys who benefit from the Earth and Metal elements, it'll be a good year to aim for that promotion you're looking for. There will be reasons to celebrate, and those could either be due to progress in career or romance, which will mark new beginnings that the Year Branch of *Chou* represents. It'll also be a good year for growth, so further your studies or learn something new, because the Earth element from the Ox zodiac gives birth to the Metal element of the Monkey zodiac.

NEGATIVE MANIFESTATIONS: Unfortunately for Monkeys who have Earth and Metal as their destructive elements, progress will be unlikely. Be careful of being lied to, and if you're promised something, it helps to be skeptical this year. Although the auxiliary star 天喜 (*tian xi*) can represent celebrations, it could also represent minor accidents, so cut down on the risky activities this year and be extra careful.

Rooster (You 酉)

Roosters have a three-harmony relationship with the Ox zodiac, which sees the strengthening of the Metal element, so people under this zodiac are expected to experience 2021 very differently from the other zodiacs. Roosters are under the influence of positive auxiliary stars representing protection (天解 *tian jie*) and abundance (禄勋 *lu xun*) and negative ones representing gossip (飞廉 *fei lian*) and physical harm (血刃 *xue ren*).

POSITIVE MANIFESTATIONS: Roosters who benefit from the Earth and Metal elements can expect an exceptional year when they'll receive a lot of help and feel very fulfilled. Existing projects and new endeavors will go smoothly, and it'll very likely be a year in which you get to reap the rewards for your efforts.

NEGATIVE MANIFESTATIONS: If Metal is a destructive element for you, the three-harmony relationship between the Branches representing the Ox and Rooster will become counterproductive. The negative auxiliary stars will likely start to take effect and your relationship with others, especially with superiors, will become strained. Minimize risky activities that might result in bodily harm.

Dog (Xu 戌)

The Branch representing the Dog zodiac has a punishment relationship with the Ox zodiac. During this process, Earth is strengthened, whereas Metal, Water, and Fire will be weakened. It will likely feel like a tumultuous year for most people under this zodiac, and whether you come out on top will be heavily dependent on whether your chart favors Earth. The Dog zodiac will be under the influence of negative auxiliary stars representing backstabbing and gossip (卷舌 *juan she*), as well as burden (绞煞 *jiao sha*), but fortunately, the auspicious star representing benefactors and protection (月德 *yue de*) comes in to mitigate things a little.

POSITIVE MANIFESTATIONS: Although a positive year is possible for people with Earth as their favorable element, the punishment relationship the Dog zodiac has with the Ox will make the journey a bumpy one. Unpleasantness and conflict are to be expected, but do not be afraid as long as you're doing something that's right and for the greater good. Remember, a punishment relationship between two zodiacs isn't intrinsically a bad thing and symbolizes the end of an element. As long as the elements being weakened are your destructive elements, the end result of whatever you go through will be a positive one.

NEGATIVE MANIFESTATIONS: Should the Earth element play a negative role in your chart, you'll need to be on your guard this year, as someone in the position of authority will abuse their power and use it against you. You are under the protection of the positive auxiliary star of 月德 (*yue de*), so make sure you seek help, and don't be afraid to protect yourself.

Pig (Hai 亥)

The Pig zodiac does not share any special relationship with the Ox, but the Earth element from Ox will still provide some pressure on people under the Pig zodiac. This is especially true when the Year Branch representing the Ox and Month Branch of the Pig both indicate winter, when growth can be difficult. The Pig zodiac is under the influence of positive auxiliary stars representing title and spiritual pursuits (太极贵人 *taiji guiren*) and wealth (金舆 *jin yu*), and negative auxiliary stars representing loss (吊客 *diao ke*).

POSITIVE MANIFESTATIONS: As two Branches representing winter will be in your chart, you'll likely need both Earth and Fire to play positive roles in order to experience a good year. If not, the excessive Water from winter will disrupt the chart's balance. People who benefit from 2021's elements can expect financial progress, but it'll come with a fair bit of travel and moving about, which will be tiring. Make sure you get credit for your work, and don't let the effort go to waste.

NEGATIVE MANIFESTATIONS: If your chart indicates that you'll experience a negative 2021 due to the imbalance of elements, it could mean that you'll likely exhaust yourself from work. The loss represented by the star 吊客 (*diao ke*) can refer to loss of your health, so please do not neglect it this year. A minority of people under the Pig zodiac will also need to watch out for their parents' health, especially if the Fire element represents either of your parents, as Fire will be put under pressure this year.

PART 2

The 10 Daymasters: 2021 for Those Born During the Year of the Ox

In the previous section, we learned what the year 2021 might hold in store for those not born under the Ox zodiac. This section lays down a general description of the ten possible Daymasters for people born in the year of the Ox and also how the seasons in which you were born will affect your chart and what elements it might need for success. This information will not apply if you were born under other zodiac signs.

Remember that no chart is perfectly balanced, so every chart will need something—an element to come into the picture to balance it. Having these balancing elements come into the picture generally means life will progress very smoothly for you in all aspects. You might find that work progresses well and your income grows steadily, your marriage is blissful, or you just feel more energized from good health.

You will read these descriptions of charts and may notice that they are being described in abstract ways, especially through comparisons with the natural world. Don't be surprised, because the Four Pillars of Destiny method was developed through these observations. These descriptions are meant to reflect the Elemental forces in your chart that indicate the negative and positive influences that will inform your year. As mentioned in the previous section, please remember this is not meant to be a forecast—it can help you as a guideline but your full chart would need to be analyzed in order for a more detailed prediction to be formed.

This section lists the Ten Heavenly Stems, representing your Daymaster, by their order, starting with Yang Wood and ending with Yin Water. Each Daymaster is further divided into four subsections representing the four seasons and the three solar months associated with it and how this changes what your chart needs. In order to find your Daymaster, visit masterseanchan .com/bazi-calculator.

Yang Wood (甲木)

Yang Wood is represented by large, majestic trees that we see in forests. This Daymaster has the ability to loosen up soil when it is too compact. Yang Wood can be carved into a valuable piece of art. It can also be processed into Fire's fuel.

SPRING

February to April
(寅, 卯, 辰) Yin / Mao / Chen. 1st to 3rd Solar Months.

If you have a Yang Wood Daymaster, this likely means that you are on the strong side. You are supported by the spring season in which you were born, and your Year Branch, represented by the Ox zodiac, grants you even more of the support you need. As a Yang Wood Daymaster born during spring, you are like an aged tree with a thick trunk and strong roots. The presence of Earth in your Year Branch will be extremely beneficial to you, because Earth gives Wood something to root itself into and from which to draw sustenance. This is the reason why Earth represents Wood's wealth.

As the Year Branch represents your parents, you will likely get immense support from your parents, especially financially. The Water hidden in the *Chou* Branch can also nourish you, while the Metal in it gives Yang Wood an opportunity to be forged into something valuable if your Elemental Phases support the strengthening of Metal. When a strong Wood is forged by Metal, the chart-holder's overall capabilities are enhanced, and this usually shows up in the ability to lead people and inspire confidence in others. Your chart quality will reach an even higher level if some Fire appears either in your natal chart or Elemental Phases, and in a balanced state relative to other elements, because that will make the environment even more conducive to Yang Wood's growth and forging.

YANG WOOD SPRING 2021: The 2021 presence of Metal and Earth will be conducive to your growth and development if you have a very strong Yang Wood Daymaster. You might find yourself being given more responsibilities and opportunities for advancement in the workplace.

SUMMER

May to July
(巳, 午, 未) Si / Wu / Wei. 4th to 6th Solar Months.

Wood loses its strength during summer and is considered to be in decline by that point. The heat of summer is a hindrance to Yang Wood's growth. The *Chou* (丑) Branch represented by your zodiac sign will play an important role in your chart in helping to keep your chart cool and moist instead of too arid. Depending on what appears in your Day and Hour Pillars, your Year Branch will likely still be able to play a constructive role in your chart, which means you will likely get support from your family.

If you were born during the fourth solar month of *Si* (May), there is a chance that a Metal combination may form when the three Branches *Chou* (丑), *Si* (巳), and *You* (酉) appear together either in your natal chart or from your Elemental Phases. This Metal combination creates too much pressure on your Yang Wood. If this happens in the chart, it is unlikely that you will get support from your family, or it will be that family starts to become less supportive the moment you reach a phase where Metal is strengthened to the point that it hurts Wood. Possible manifestations include having your attention to goals diverted by the challenges your parents are facing. These problems could be due to their health or financial problems. Whether they come from the father or mother depends on what Metal represents in your chart. If this Metal combination is built within your natal chart, it would mean that you were born into a harsh environment not conducive to your growth, so elements that may be able to remedy this combination will need to appear.

YANG WOOD SUMMER 2021: The 2021 impact on your life will depend on whether the Metal element plays a positive role in your chart. Metal's presence is best coupled with Water's, and these elements represent the Officer and Resource God, respectively. They can represent significant progress in career and influence when they appear together.

AUTUMN

August to October
(申, 酉, 戌) Shen / You / Xu. 7th to 9th Solar Months.

Not only does Wood not get any form of support during autumn, the nature of the Yin Earth Branch, *Chou*, will strengthen Metal even further. Such a chart structure does suggest a lack of support from family, and you may have been born into a harsh environment. Achievements during the early part of your life may be limited, especially in academics.

A Wood chart born with so much Metal will definitely need remedying elements, which in this case would be Water, so that Wood can be protected from Metal by preventing a clash. As Water represents your mother, your affinity with her will be higher, and she will play a vital role in your growth and development. However, Water must appear either in your natal chart or Elemental Phases in a strong manner and not come under harm by opposing elements. The absence of Water here gives Metal a chance to overpower Wood, which will usually manifest as health ailments and obstacles in the form of harsh environments, and this could be in your workplace or even family.

YANG WOOD AUTUMN 2021: The presence of Water will be critical for a chart like this. If Water is absent, then the appearance of Metal and Earth in 2021 will add a lot of pressure to Yang Wood, and it does not symbolize a year of growth for the chart-holder.

WINTER

November to January
(亥, 子, 丑) Hai / Zi / Chou. 10th to 12th Solar Months.

Although Water gives birth to Wood, theoretically speaking, Water itself must be in the right state in order to achieve this. As both your Year Branch and Month Branch represent the winter season, your chart would be considered far too cold for Yang Wood to grow healthfully. There is also a risk of Water combinations forming, as two out of the three Water Branches are now present, so the risk of your Yang Wood becoming driftwood due to the torrents forming in your chart is high. In other words, Yang Wood's value and use will be removed in the presence of too much Water. If you find that your chart has excessive Water, it's important not to end up a drifter and having a lethargic or lackadaisical approach to life.

The Earth element is particularly important in a chart like yours, but take note that Dry Earth or Yang Earth is preferred, because these Branches are the ones that can address the problem of too much Water in your chart. Wet Earth does not help with this. If the Earth element is missing in a Water-dominated chart, you'll find that wealth would be extremely difficult to acquire due to the limitations you've set yourself.

YANG WOOD WINTER 2021: The 2021 influence on you will likely depend on whether you have Fire elements in your chart to strengthen Earth, so that it can remove the excessive Water in your natal chart.

Yin Wood (乙木)

Yin Wood is represented by small plants like shrubs, herbs, and grass. Despite being a Wood element like Yang Wood, Yin Wood's use and role in nature are very different. It is more vulnerable to the environment, and strict conditions need to be met in order for Yin Wood to grow well.

SPRING

February to April
(寅, 卯, 辰). Yin / Mao / Chen. 1st to 3rd Solar Months.

Both your Year Branch and Month Branch provide ample support to your Yin Wood, and it's possible that your Yin Wood will become a strong plant. The question is whether your Yin Wood's strength will be sustained so it can continue growing. Yin Wood in this state welcomes Fire to aid in its continued growth, because it is already being supplied Earth and Water via the Year Branch of *Chou*.

The *Chou* Branch is not as conducive to Yin Wood's growth on its own without the support of other elements. As such, the influence your family has on you will be a positive one, but the help they can render you will be limited. It will be important for you to encounter the Fire element somewhere in your natal chart or during your Elemental Phases—your chart is likely that of a late bloomer. Additional Wood and Water elements will manifest as lack of personal growth and even a hostile environment if Wood and Water become excessive.

YIN WOOD SPRING 2021: Your Yin Wood Daymaster will likely be in a strong state in 2021, especially if your Day Pillar or Hour Pillar has Wood or Water elements.

The 2021 elements will likely benefit you, as the Year Branch of *Chou* will give Yin Wood something to root itself into to grow, although the best situation would also include the presence of Fire.

SUMMER

May to July
(巳, 午, 未) Si / Wu / Wei. 4th to 6th Solar Months.

The Water hidden in the *Chou* Branch combined with the warmth of summer gives Yin Wood an excellent environment to grow. However, Fire is the dominant element in this chart, as you were born during summer, so the environment is considered arid and will require adjustment. This is likely a chart where Water is required. Contrary to popular belief, Yin Wood grows the most during the Fire season represented by summer instead of a Water season represented by winter because Yin Wood perishes much more quickly from drowning under Water than it does from heat. The key to the quality of such a chart is to look at whether Water is present. If Water appears to balance the conditions in the chart, the chart-holder will be blessed with progress and protection in life and will do very well academically too. The lack of Water, on the other hand, symbolizes being in a harsh environment that drains the chart-holder's emotional well-being and health.

A chart structure like this can be more volatile and prone to sudden changes if the Metal combination formed by *Chou* 丑, *Si* 巳, and *You* 酉 ever appears in the chart. Unlike Yang Wood, Yin Wood is not meant to be carved, so an overpowering presence of Metal causes Yin Wood to break, which will manifest as the chart-holder lacking the capability to do well in life and thrive.

YIN WOOD SUMMER 2021: The 2021 influence on your life will depend on whether Water exists in your chart. The presence of Water allows you to benefit from Yin Metal appearing in 2021, because Metal helps to strengthen Water, which will in turn strengthen your Yin Wood Daymaster. However, if Water is completely absent from your chart, elements of 2021 will likely harm you.

AUTUMN

August to October
(申, 酉, 戌) Shen / You / Xu. 7th to 9th Solar Months.

Yin Wood will be at its absolute weakest during autumn, and the Wet Earth Branch of *Chou* will end up strengthening the presence of Metal coming from the season you were born in. A chart structure like this paints a picture of Yin Wood trying to survive in a harsh environment. Metal does not bring out the best in Yin Wood, as Yin Wood is not meant to be carved or forged by Metal. It is meant to be nourished by the balanced state of Earth, Water, and Fire.

Excessive Metal needs to be addressed by bringing in remedying elements either in the natal chart or Elemental Phases, which can be done in a few ways. Either Water can come in between Metal and Wood to prevent a clash, or Fire can appear to weaken Metal. This allows the chart-holder to tap into the positive side of Metal, which would represent leadership ability. If that does not happen, progress in life will be a lot harder, as Yin Wood isn't allowed to grow in such harsh conditions, and this will reflect the state of the chart-holder's growth as well. Female charts may also experience difficulties in relationships if the presence of excessive Metal isn't addressed, so it's better to wait until you're in a Water or Fire phase before you consider settling down, rather than rushing into a marriage before that.

YIN WOOD AUTUMN 2021: It is paramount that one's chart have Water. If not, the Yin Metal from 2021 will end up harming the chart-holder, and it'll likely turn out to be a very challenging year.

WINTER

November to January
(亥, 子, 丑) Hai / Zi / Chou. 10th to 12th Solar Months.

The winter season is gentler on Yin Wood compared to autumn, but this chart will be too cold, as you were born during winter. As both the Year Branch and Month Branch are now winter Branches, Yin Wood's growth is impeded, which is a scenario you'll see in nature. Plants do not grow during winter and the most they can do is to survive in a harsh environment. Additional Wood elements in the natal chart would not help Yin Wood grow—this only helps it to stay alive and endure until the season passes. For growth to happen, the environment needs to change, which means that you'll need to encounter a Fire Ten-Year Phase in order to get rid of the coldness of winter, and this will most likely happen by your middle age as you progress to later Ten-Year Phases. Together with Earth and Water—which already exist in this chart in the Year and Month Branch—the three elements of Earth, Water, and Fire give Yin Wood a conducive environment for growth.

As winter and the Water element aren't as harmful, the negative effect on Yin Wood is a more indirect and subtle one, unlike Metal's, which is more direct. If additional Water is coming into the picture from your natal chart or Elemental Phases, the environment you will find yourself in will negatively impact you in a way that you may not realize, so try to be cognizant of that and remove yourself from negative situations as much as possible.

YIN WOOD WINTER 2021: The 2021 year will likely be one of growth and progress, but you may feel sluggish in spite of it, because the Branch representing the Ox zodiac is a winter Branch. Yin Metal, which appears in 2021, is not welcomed here either. The critical element required for a fortuitous year is Fire.

Yang Fire (丙火)

Yang Fire represents a blazing inferno, the kind that we might find in furnaces. Its value can only be realized if it is burning with sufficient strength while also in a controlled state. Yang Fire can also be used to represent the sun's presence, and it is seen as the appropriate element to remove the cold so that life can flourish.

SPRING

February to April
(寅, 卯, 辰). Yin / Mao / Chen. 1st to 3rd Solar Months.

Yang Fire during spring is like a wildfire waiting to ignite. The role your zodiac sign plays will be different depending on the elements that appear in other parts of the chart.

If your chart is overwhelmed by additional Fire and Wood elements, do guard against being too strong-headed or stubborn and imposing your views and perspective on others. It is also extremely important for you to be in the right company because any additional Fire appearing in your chart will manifest as people likely to harm you or wish to benefit from you at your expense. In such a situation, your Wet Earth Ox zodiac sign will play a very constructive and meaningful role in your chart by controlling the strength of Fire, so it is important to allow your family to play that positive role in your life.

YANG FIRE SPRING 2021: Your Yang Fire Daymaster is likely a strong one. As such, the Metal and Wet Earth appearing in 2021 will play a positive role in your chart to ensure it stays in a balanced state. As Metal here represents wealth, financial progress and new opportunities are very likely.

SUMMER

May to July

(巳, 午, 未) Si / Wu / Wei. 4th to 6th Solar Months.

Summer is the period during which Yang Fire metaphorically goes out of control. During this time, achieving balance in the chart is important. This can be done in a few ways, usually using either Wet Earth or Water, depending on how one's chart is structured. Earth drains Fire gently, while Water controls Fire directly. If you use Water, it needs to appear with enough strength—if not, its presence will actually make things worse. If Earth appears, ideally it is Wet Earth instead of Dry Earth. Note that Water and Earth should not appear at the same time, as that produces an unnecessary clash between the possible beneficial elements. The focus should only be on one.

If you were born during the sixth solar month of *Wei* (July), Fire will not be as strong in your chart. Your Year Branch of *Chou* (丑) will clash with your Month Branch of *Wei* (未), which will significantly dissipate Fire's strength. In this case, Wood may be required to further strengthen Fire. Your early life and career may experience lots of changes as a result of this clash, but things should stabilize by middle age.

YANG FIRE SUMMER 2021: How 2021 will go depends on whether you were born during the fourth, fifth, or sixth solar months (May, June, or July). If you were born during the fourth or fifth solar month, your Yang Fire Daymaster is likely already strong, so the Wet Earth that appears in 2021 will be beneficial for you. In this case, it will manifest as a period during which you will enjoy the fruit of your labor and a time when your emotional well-being will be enhanced.

AUTUMN

August to October
(申, 酉, 戌) Shen / You / Xu. 7th to 9th Solar Months.

At this stage, Yang Fire is in a state of decline during the season dominated by Metal. The *Chou* Branch that your zodiac represents contributes to Metal's strength, making Yang Fire even weaker. Wood and Fire will need to appear in your natal chart or Elemental Phases to address this weakness. If they do not, wealth acquisition and career advancement will likely pose as challenges throughout life and not come easily to you because your Yang Fire will not be strong enough to do its job of forging Metal—which represents Fire's wealth.

Your Year Branch and Month Branch do not clash with each other, so drastic changes in the early stages of your life are unlikely, and your family environment is probably a rather stable one as well. Pay close attention to the Wood element–it is critical in your chart and represents your mother. If the Wood element is harmed by excessive Metal, it will likely manifest as issues and difficulties faced by your mother. In addition, if you have a chart in which Metal clashes excessively with Wood, you will need to pay close attention to your relationship with money and finances. Make sure your desire to acquire wealth is motivated by just, noble causes and not for the sake of money itself.

YANG FIRE AUTUMN 2021: Ideally, you are in a Wood Ten-Year Phase, which would mean that your Yang Fire is getting some support. If not, make sure you are always seeking ways to improve yourself, especially by gaining new knowledge, as Wood represents academic interests and the pursuit of knowledge.

WINTER

November to January
(亥, 子, 丑) Hai / Zi / Chou. 10th to 12th Solar Months.

Yang Fire is at risk of being harmed during the winter season due to the presence of Water. The stronger the presence of Water, the weaker Yang Fire becomes, and this, naturally, has negative implications for the chart-holder. When your Daymaster has to struggle to exist, what manifests in real life will have its own parallels, and you will experience difficulties in several areas of your life. Yang Fire represents the sun, and the sun represents a strong presence and influence, so a struggling Yang Fire Daymaster suggests that it's hard for you to be noticed or recognized. A chart like this will need a strong presence of Wood to protect Fire from Water; by being separated by Wood, Water and Fire are prevented from clashing directly.

If you are Yang Fire, your success will be highly dependent on whether you are able to truly earn the respect of others and whether you have what it takes to be in a position of power and authority. The Water element appears as your Officer God, which represents status and authority, but to wield such power takes a strong, wise person. Having a strong Daymaster supported by Wood means you have what it takes to wield such power and authority. A focus on personal growth is extremely important in a chart like yours. Do not let the difficulties you encounter turn into resentment.

YANG FIRE SUMMER 2021: The elements that appear in 2021 do not favor you, because Metal harms Wood, and Wet Earth strengthens Metal, so 2021 will likely be a year when progress will be a lot more difficult—but you can look forward to 2022, when we'll enter the Wood phase of the twelve-year zodiac cycle, which will be a more auspicious time for you.

Yin Fire (丁火)

Yin Fire represents a small, controlled flame like that of a candle. It represents the Fire we use in day-to-day life. Although it is less effective at removing the coldness of winter, Yin Fire's value comes from the fact that it can be easily controlled and put to use, especially in the forging of Metal. The quality of Yin Fire charts is determined by whether Yin Fire can burn in a controlled and sustainable manner.

SPRING

February to April
(寅, 卯, 辰). Yin / Mao / Chen. 1st to 3rd Solar Months.

The mere existence of Wood during spring will neither support nor strengthen Yin Fire. Yin Fire is a small flame, and dumping too much Wood on it would suffocate it. The theory of Yin, Yang, and the Five Elements states that Wood needs to be processed by Metal in order for it to be used effectively to empower Yin Fire. In layman's terms, you need to chop a tree into logs to turn it into firewood—you cannot just throw the tree onto a fire and expect it to burn. It may feel a bit counterintuitive, but a chart like yours will welcome Metal, as it actually helps Yin Fire to continue to burn in the presence of Wood.

Every Stem, or Daymaster, has a corresponding Wealth Vault represented by an Earth Branch. The Branch that represents the Ox zodiac is a little special in your case, as it also represents your Wealth Vault, as the *Chou* Branch constrains Metal, and Metal represents Fire's wealth. It represents a lot of financial support coming from your family, especially if the Metal element also appears in other parts of your chart. Pay special attention to the balance between Wood and Metal.

YIN FIRE SPRING 2021: The 2021 influence on you can go in either direction, depending on whether your chart needs more Wood or has enough of it already. If your chart happens to have additional Wood appearing in the Day or Hour Pillars, The 2021 elements will generally be supportive, especially for career.

SUMMER

May to July
(巳, 午, 未) Si / Wu / Wei. 4th to 6th Solar Months.

Yin Fire during summer shares similarities with Yang Fire during summer; Fire burns in an uncontrolled state during summer and its use cannot be harnessed. As such, the priority here is to make Yin Fire controllable.

If you were born during the fourth or fifth solar months (May or June) when Fire is at its peak, you will need to weaken Yin Fire using opposing elements—for example, you could use either Water or Wet Earth, but not both at the same time. Your Year Branch will play a very vital role in ensuring balance in your chart, because Wet Earth can control Yin Fire's strength.

If you were born during the sixth solar month of *Wei* (July), Fire will already be in decline, and Yin Fire will not be in a strong state. The clash between *Chou* and *Wei* will also further weaken Yin Fire. In this case, Wood is required to remove the excess Earth so that Yin Fire can breathe. In this process, you'll see potential you never knew you had being unleashed.

YIN FIRE SUMMER 2021: Similar to a Yang Fire chart, how 2021 turns out will be highly dependent on the solar month during which you were born. If you were born during the peak Fire months of the fourth and fifth, 2021 will be a very positive year for you.

AUTUMN

August to October
(申, 酉, 戌) Shen / You / Xu. 7th to 9th Solar Months.

Yin Fire is considered weak once autumn arrives. During spring, a Yin Fire welcomes Metal, and similarly, a Yin Fire during autumn welcomes Wood. Metal and Wood come together to give Yin Wood a constant source of fuel and sustenance. Your Year Branch here will likely not play a positive role in your chart, signifying that you may have had a tougher start to life and little financial and emotional support from parents.

The quality of your chart is heavily dependent on the existence of Wood. If Wood is present, your chart will generally signify success, indicating that wealth and status will eventually appear—in particular, whenever you reach a Wood Elemental Phase. The Wood element manifests as the Resource God, representing status, authority, and possibly a position of power. The key to success in such charts is that the chart-holders must maintain their moral authority and not take their status and authority for granted. They must put their power to use for the benefit of others. People with such charts in feudal China often ended up working in government, but nowadays this could refer to a high-level corporate position. It's important that no clashes or harm come to any Wood element appearing in your chart, as this would form a taboo structure in Bazi theory. People with this taboo chart structure tend to pursue wealth at the expense of others and the greater good, and may get into trouble due to this. In other words, people with such charts should not be greedy and overstep boundaries, especially legal ones.

YIN FIRE AUTUMN 2021: The 2021 Metal and Earth are elements that you will not need, so it's unlikely to be a smooth sailing year for you. You're better off being spending the year consolidating your plans and efforts to ensure a better year in 2022.

WINTER

November to January
(亥, 子, 丑) Hai / Zi / Chou. 10th to 12th Solar Months.

Yin Fire is, as you might expect, weak during the winter season, and it is a lot more vulnerable than Yang Fire to being extinguished by Water, so protecting it from Water is important. The cycle of birth for the elements allows Wood to absorb Water and convert it into Fire. This ensures that Fire doesn't end up getting extinguished. Take a close look at your chart and pay careful attention to the period when you enter into a Wood phase; that would be considered your turning point and when your life may begin improving. You might start a new job in a new industry or you may begin learning something new that eventually turns into your livelihood.

Your Year Branch is also regarded as your Wealth Vault because *Chou* holds Metal, which represents Fire's wealth, but this Wealth Vault will only be of use to you if Yin Fire is well supported and able to survive the pressure from Water. If your Daymaster is strong enough, your Ox zodiac Year Branch will manifest as a lot of financial support from your family, so look out for additional Wood or Fire elements in your natal chart.

YIN FIRE WINTER 2021: The 2021 elements will likely put pressure on you because your Yin Fire Daymaster is likely on the weak side already, so additional Metal and Earth won't help in this case. As Metal represents wealth for a Fire person, it's likely to be a year when financial pressure will arise and you may find yourself not earning enough to support your current lifestyle or service your debts. A rule of thumb to remember is that whenever the wealth element gets too strong, it overburdens the chart-holder and the chart-holder ends up having to chase after wealth.

Yang Earth (戊土)

Immovable and rock-solid, Yang Earth's nature is hard and dry. It is not the kind of soil that you use for agriculture, but rather the kind you see enclosing large sources of water, like streams, rivers, and lakes. Yang Earth demonstrates its value when it is not *too* compact and dry, and it often needs Wood and Water elements to achieve this.

SPRING

February to April
(寅, 卯, 辰). Yin / Mao / Chen. 1st to 3rd Solar Months.

Earth during Spring is weak, as Wood, which is dominant during spring, will control Earth. But take special note that spring is also the season in which, just before summer, Yang Earth's growth begins. With the right supporting elements, Earth *can* still thrive during spring, but it will need Fire to support its continued growth.

Being under the Ox zodiac, your Year Branch is an Earth Branch, which contributes to the strength of Yang Earth, but only a little. The *Chou* Branch represents a period when Yang Earth is still in its infancy. So, despite being an Earth Branch, this year will not automatically push Yang Earth into a state of being strong. Fire will still be required here, as it will give your chart the extra push it needs to let Yang Earth be in a strong state. You'll need Fire to appear in other parts of your natal chart or your Elemental Phases. Fire represents your Resource God, so its presence in your chart will be a reflection of how much knowledge you can acquire and whether you'll able to use it to put yourself in a position of authority. If your chart lacks Fire, it will be important for you to equip yourself with the necessary knowledge and skill to thrive wherever you are.

The presence of Fire in your chart allows your Yang Earth Daymaster to tap into the effects of the Wood element, which represents your Officer God. In other words, if Fire is present in your chart, you will belong to a group of people with exceptional leadership qualities. Success will not come from the direct pursuit of wealth, but rather, through your reputation and good social standing.

YANG EARTH SPRING 2021: The 2021 year elements and influence on you will be highly dependent on the state and strength of your Daymaster, so look out for additional Fire and Earth elements in your chart. If the presence of Fire and Earth become overwhelming, the additional Earth from 2021 will be a burden on your chart, resulting in possible wealth loss.

SUMMER

May to July
(巳, 午, 未) Si / Wu / Wei. 4th to 6th Solar Months.

Yang Earth during summer is too dry and arid, which causes its value to diminish. The rule of thumb for Yang Earth people born during summer is to look for Water to alter the environment their chart depicts. Ideally, they'll also add some Wood to loosen up the Yang. Wood extending its roots to break up Earth is akin to an Earth person accepting someone else's presence and thoughts. So when Earth is too strong and without Wood, it manifests as the chart-holder being stubborn and unwilling to accept another person's perspective.

Your Year Branch of *Chou* is Wet Earth. Water is already weakening, so it does not help summer's Yang Earth much, as the presence of Water is not strong enough to mitigate summer's heat and dryness. If you were born during the sixth solar month of *Wei* (July), special attention must be paid to your family, as the clashes between your Year Branch and Month Branch remove beneficial elements that might have been supplied by a strong familial relationship. A clash like this suggests difficulties faced by your parents, especially your father.

YANG EARTH SUMMER 2021: The 2021 year effects on your life greatly depend on whether Water already exists in your natal chart. If Water appears in your chart in a meaningful form, with sufficient strength and without being harmed by outside elements, 2021 is a year when progress can be achieved if you try hard enough. Just be patient, because it will likely happen in the third and fourth quarters of the year.

AUTUMN

August to October
(申, 酉, 戌) Shen / You / Xu. 7th to 9th Solar Months.

Yang Earth's strength begins to decline during the season of autumn as Metal's dominance starts to set in. Your Year Branch of *Chou* will help your weak Yang Daymaster a little but not sufficiently to completely counteract that weakness. If you were born during the seventh or eighth solar months (August or September), the Output Gods Hurting Officer and Eating God will appear. The positive sides of these Gods do not show up unless your Daymaster is strong, so instead of manifesting as wealth and creative output, they indicate a chart-holder who may be leaning toward naivete and complacency. Fire must appear in this chart to balance the effect of this tendency and imbue the chart-holder with a strong sense of purpose and responsibility. If you find Fire lacking in your chart, observe whether you take life too easily and whether you have goals set for yourself, as you might be taking everything a bit too leisurely. This happens when one's Daymaster is being drained excessively, which in this case is Earth being drained by Metal as Metal relies on Earth to grow.

If you were born during the ninth solar month of *Xu* (October), which is an Earth month, Yang Earth does start to lean toward the strong side and become too dense and compact, which is also a sign of Yang Earth's value diminishing. In this case, your chart will be similar to a summer Yang Earth chart in which Earth, because it is too strong, will require Wood. The lack of Wood in that case may manifest as a lack of abundance both financially and emotionally, especially due to *Chou* Branch and *Xu* Branch's destructive relations with each other. Chart-holders with this will likely end up in a harsh family environment with parents ending up being a burden, or chart-holders might often find themselves at the mercy of authority figures who abuse their power.

YANG EARTH AUTUMN 2021: People born during the ninth solar month of *Xu* (October) will need to pay special attention to their chart, as Yang Earth starts to become too strong and compact, meaning Yang Earth is in a low-quality state. The 2021 year's effects on such a chart will be mixed as Earth starts to become excessive and the quality and state of Earth diminish due to the imbalance of elements.

WINTER

November to January
(亥, 子, 丑) Hai / Zi / Chou. 10th to 12th Solar Months.

Earth and Water have a unique relationship with each other. When both of these elements are of equal strength, they come together to form a pond, lake, or river, and play a meaningful role in nature as a nourisher of life. However, if either element overpowers the other, this positive state cannot exist. When Water is too strong, it completely washes Earth away, and Water cannot be contained and used in a productive way. But if Earth is too strong, it will suck Water completely dry, and there will be nothing to use.

During winter Yang Earth is weakest and Water is at its strongest. There is a risk of not being able to be held together by Earth, which manifests as the chart-holder's inability to acquire and hold on to wealth. Even though your Year Branch is of Earth, it is not considered a strong source of it, as *Chou* represents Earth at its infancy stages when it is not strong yet. Furthermore, a Water combination formed by *Hai, Zi, and Chou* may likely form as a result. When Water becomes too strong, Earth is washed away, and this represents a situation in which the chart-holder feels constantly overwhelmed, resulting in lack of focus and crumbling under pressure. Should you find excessive Water in your chart, you'll either need to improve your capacity for handling pressure or ask yourself whether the effort you're putting into whatever you do is worth the returns.

Additional Earth is important in a chart like this, as it represents good company and people who will be able to help you. If the Elemental Phases are against you, Yang Earth chart-holders with excessive Water may often feel overwhelmed by episodes of depression, so surrounding yourself with the right people is even more important. With each new phase comes a different environment, and your environment will eventually change for the better with supportive people around you. Such charts also indicate late bloomers, and the early, formative years are critical if you wish to make the most of the middle age.

YANG EARTH WINTER 2021: The 2021 Branch of Wet Earth does not provide Yang Earth with enough support, as the Year Branch of *Chou* is not where Yang Earth is the strongest. As Water represents Earth's wealth, 2021 will likely be a year when the return on one's efforts, especially monetarily and career-wise, may be below expectations.

Yin Earth (己土)

As the opposite of hard and dry Yang Earth, Yin Earth is wet and loose. It is the kind of soil that we can put to use easily, not just in agriculture, but in construction as well. It nourishes other living beings and elements as easily as it dissipates. Yin Earth is more resilient during summer, as it carries some moisture, but it is more susceptible to being washed away by Water during winter when Water is dominant.

SPRING

February to April
(寅, 卯, 辰). Yin / Mao / Chen. 1st to 3rd Solar Months.

Yin Earth is more susceptible to Wood's control, as its nature contrasts Yang Earth's, being a softer, less-firm form of Earth. If Yang Earth needs Fire during spring to protect and strengthen it, then Yin Earth would need it even more.

Similar to Yang Earth, if Fire appears to support to Yin Earth, the chart-holder will naturally be able to tap into what Wood represents, which is leadership, authority, and status. That being said, the Yin Earth person's approach to life and the way they handle things is different from a Yang Earth person. Yin Earth's leadership style encompasses a subtlety that Yang Earth does not have. You'll likely find Yin Earth people a bit more nurturing, whereas Yang Earth people are more often led by their principles and can appear stricter.

If you were born during the third solar month of *Chen* (April) when Earth is dominant, your Yin Earth has the benefit of a lot of support, which will manifest in the possibility of receiving a lot of help from peers, as well as the capacity to acquire wealth. However, balance still needs to be maintained, so if additional Fire or Earth appears in other parts of the chart, then the chart-holder needs elements like Metal and Water to drain Yin Earth's strength in order to keep the chart balanced. If Earth's presence starts to become overwhelming, it will begin to show its negative side and will represent wealth loss and competition instead.

YIN EARTH SPRING 2021: The effects of 2021's elements on a Yin Earth Daymaster chart-holder will really depend on the state of the chart. People born during the first and second solar months (February and March) will benefit, as Earth is likely required. However, if enough Earth and Fire exists to push the Daymaster to the strong side, then 2021 will come with some difficulties, such as increased competition.

SUMMER

May to July
(巳, 午, 未) Si / Wu / We. 4th to 6th Solar Months.

Yin Earth shares an issue with Yang Earth during summer, which is the risk of Earth, be it Yin or Yang, becoming too dry and arid. Yin Earth is considerably more resilient in summer compared to Yang Earth, as Yin Earth is considered Wet Earth, allowing it to retain a bit of its value during summer.

That being said, Yin Earth still needs the presence of Water, Yin Water in particular, during the summer season for it to retain its value, so if you are a Yin Earth Summer, you should still be looking for the presence of Water in your chart. Similarly, Water represents Yin Earth's wealth, so Water appearing in a chart like this does indicate that the chart-holder will be effective in acquiring wealth. Do take note that the overall chart structure must still be balanced and the appearance of Water should be of equal strength instead of overpowering Fire and Earth. Water overpowering Fire or Earth manifests as the chart-holder's inability to cope with pressure and grow. In other words, progress in career and wealth might come at the expense of your health and emotional well-being. Look out for Branch combinations that strengthen Water, especially when *Hai* (亥), *Zi* (子), and *Chou* (丑) appear together.

YIN EARTH SUMMER 2021: If your chart already has Water in it, 2021 will be an excellent year, as the Metal from 2021 will help strengthen Water and help keep your chart in a balanced state by making sure summer's Fire does not diminish Earth's value.

AUTUMN

August to October
(申, 酉, 戌) Shen / You / Xu. 7th to 9th Solar Months.

Autumn and winter are when Yin Earth is weaker than Yang Earth, because the climate is starting to become cold. Given that Yin Earth is the wet, colder version of Earth, a cold climate will bring down Yin Earth's value more than Yang Earth, which is a dry, warmer form of Earth.

Yin Earth during autumn requires more Fire than Yang Earth does, because Yin Earth turns colder faster. As such, if you are a Yin Earth person born during autumn without any Fire in your chart, your character flaws will be a lot more pronounced than a Yang Earth person's, and you will need to address them more forcefully in order to achieve success. The exception is a Yin Earth person born during the ninth solar month of *Xu* (October) when Earth is dominant, which helps to strengthen Yin Earth. As both the Year Branch and Month Branch are now Earth, which makes Yin Earth more compact, your chart will require some Wood to come in to loosen it and have its value extracted, and for the positive character traits of both Earth and Wood to manifest. Similar to a Yang Earth chart-holder, an excessively strong Yin Earth chart results in a person who tends to be stubborn and unable to take in other perspectives. However, the difference is that a too-strong Yin Earth chart-holder will not make this tendency known and will instead disagree with you quietly.

YIN EARTH AUTUMN 2021: The Yin Earth Daymaster people who are likely benefit most from 2021 are those born during the ninth solar month of *Xu (October)*. Earth gets excessively strong in this month, and the most effective way of remedying excessive Earth is to use Metal to drain it. The 2021 year's Yin Metal will provide that element, so 2021 will be mixed in terms of success, but inclined toward positive for those born in the ninth solar month. Still, they'll most likely have a better year than people who are born during the seventh and eighth solar months (August and September).

WINTER

November to January
(亥, 子, 丑) Hai / Zi / Chou. 10th to 12th Solar Months.

Winter is the season when Yin Earth's value is at its lowest, because Yin Earth is far too cold to nourish any form of life or be used in any constructive way. On top of that, Yin Earth is also at the risk of being washed away by the Water element, which is dominant during winter. Fire is definitely needed for a Yin Earth born during winter, and Yin Earth needs it much more than Yang Earth does. Your Year Branch of *Chou*, despite being an Earth Branch, will not help here, since its position does not represent a period when Yin Earth is strong. Earth is only strongest during summer, which is at least four solar months away.

Yin Earth can be washed away by Water much more easily than Yang Earth, so expect the negative effects of having excessive Water to be greater for Yin Earth individuals. Excessive Water will cause the chart-holder to feel constantly overwhelmed. Any wealth acquisition will usually come at the expense of another aspect of your life, so make sure you pay attention to work–life balance and don't neglect your health and family. Learning how to balance various aspects of your life will be incredibly important in this case for charts like yours.

YIN EARTH WINTER: The year 2021 will be a sluggish one for Yin Earth Winter chart-holders, as Yin Earth will likely become overwhelmed by Water. If you have this chart, you will be unlikely to feel drive or ambition to achieve great things due to Yin Earth being drained excessively by Metal and not getting enough support from either Fire or Earth. Take this time to learn something new and network, because you'll likely need to wait until the Fire part of the twelve-year zodiac cycle ends to progress—and that won't happen until 2025.

Yang Metal (庚金)

Yang Metal is like a strong Metal ore ready to be forged. Yang Metal is hard in nature, and it is the kind of Metal that is used to make weapons or tools. However, before it can be used, it has to be forged by Fire. The question that always revolves around Yang Metal is whether it can survive the forging process, and if it can, whether Yin Fire and Yang Wood will be around to provide the forging conditions. In other words, Yang Metal, Yin Fire, and Yang Wood have a very special relationship with one another, and you'll always see them mentioned together. Yang Metal is the tool required to process Yang Wood into firewood; Yin Fire is the flame required to forge Yang Metal. These three elements are part of what is called a virtuous cycle.

SPRING

February to April
(寅, 卯, 辰). Yin / Mao / Chen. 1st to 3rd Solar Months.

Although Metal is weakest during the season of spring, your Year Branch will play a unique role in supporting Yang Metal. Your zodiac sign, represented by the *Chou* Branch, will not only strengthen Yang Metal, but also protect it from Fire. What this also means is that we can safely bring in Fire to forge Yang Metal, and this is important, because Fire brings out the best in Yang Metal. As your Daymaster is weak, 2021 will be a year when you'll receive help and be able to achieve a lot as you receive assistance from 2021's Earth and Metal elements.

You likely come from a very supportive family due to your Year Branch, but this support needs to be leveraged correctly. Metaphorically and astrologically speaking, the appearance of Wood and Fire in a chart structured like yours means that you will eventually be forged into a valuable tool or weapon. If Wood is negatively affected or Fire does not appear, Metal will remain an ore, a state in which it cannot be effectively used. To put it simply: Do not see a comfortable, unchallenging environment as a good thing, because you will be missing out on a lot of valuable opportunities to become a better, stronger person.

YANG METAL SPRING 2021: The year 2021 will be very supportive for most Yang Metal Daymaster holders, as many of these charts will likely need some strengthening from Metal and Earth, which will be present throughout 2021. Financial progress and higher income can be expected.

SUMMER

May to July
(巳, 午, 未) Si / Wu / Wei. 4th to 6th Solar Months.

Summer is usually risky for Yang Metal, as summer is associated with Fire. Fire, as much as it is useful in forging Metal, can also harm it. Summertime is not a period when Yang Metal is ready to be forged, so supporting elements are necessary to ensure the Fire of summer does not end up melting Metal but forms it into useful materials instead. Your zodiac sign, represented by your Year Branch, will play a very important role in your chart, as it protects your Yang Metal from Fire. With a supportive Year Branch of Wet Earth represented by Ox, Fire is in a good position to do its job and form Yang Metal. As Fire manifests as your Officer God, your chart indicates that you'll be someone imbued with leadership qualities, so positions of authority should be an eventuality the moment you enter into a positive Ten-Year Phase, which will likely be an Earth or Metal Phase. A Bazi calculator will be able point this out, as it maps out all the Ten-Year Phases you're destined to go through.

Yang Metal chart-holders born during the fourth or fifth solar months (May or June) are still likely to need Metal and Earth in their charts, as Fire represents a season in which Yang Metal is still very weak. The 2021 year's Earth and Metal elements will be very beneficial for these people, so career progress can be expected, but more in the form of reputation, power, and title and not on the monetary side.

Do take note if you are born during the sixth solar month of *Wei* (July) as Fire's strength will have diminished and Earth will start to get a bit excessive. In this case, the requirements for a higher quality chart change as well. Wood will become a requirement for success. The 2021 year's elements will likely not benefit Yang Metal people born during the sixth solar month, as additional Metal and Earth are no longer necessary.

YANG METAL SUMMER 2021: People born during the fourth and fifth solar months (May and June) will benefit the most from 2021's elements, as Earth and Metal are likely required for success. For people born during the sixth solar month, for a positive year, you'll need Wood to appear in your natal chart or Elemental Phases to balance out Earth and Metal's strength. If not, the year will be full of financial pressures.

AUTUMN

August to October
(申, 酉, 戌) Shen / You / Xu. 7th to 9th Solar Months.

Autumn is the season when Metal is at its strongest. The change of the seasons completely alters the role and impact the Year Branch has on your chart. As Metal is already in a strong state, the *Chou* Branch represented by your zodiac sign is considered excessive and begins to become a burden. It paints a picture of Yang Metal as an unrefined ore that has no constructive use in its current state. Fire is desperately needed to extract Yang Metal's value. Should Wood appear in a chart like this without the presence of Fire, you will have to watch out for the well-being of your father, as he is represented by Wood.

A strong Yang Metal chart that does not go through forging by Fire is like a metal ore that has not been processed. It is not forged into a tool that can be used and has no value. Manifested into real life, the chart-holder will find him- or herself with little to offer, so progress in terms of career and finances will be very limited. A strong emphasis on growing through setbacks and difficulties is important for charts structured like this, and it is a trait that is unique to Yang Metal charts. In other words, Yang Metal people need to go through trial by fire. Growth needs to come from discomfort and challenges. The presence of Wood and Fire appearing together will be extremely important for such charts because without it, Yang Metal is no different from scrap metal and it will manifest in character flaws such as a tendency to react negatively to challenges instead of learning from them.

YANG METAL AUTUMN 2021: It's unlikely that 2021 will be a positive year for Yang Metal people born during these months, as the Yin Metal and Wet Earth in their charts are both destructive elements at a time when Earth is already in excess. You will likely find yourself feeling lethargic and unwilling to improve, and the chances of losing your source of wealth will be high too. It is important to always remind yourself that challenges and adversities exist to help you grow and get more out of your life.

WINTER

November to January
(亥, 子, 丑) Hai / Zi / Chou. 10th to 12th Solar Months.

Metal begins its decline during winter, and Water, which is associated with winter, drains Metal's strength. On top of that, Water does not forge Yang Metal, and you cannot hammer Yang Metal into a tool or weapon using Water—you need Fire. A strong presence of Earth and Fire is required to get rid of Water in this case. Your Year Branch plays no constructive role in your chart during this season despite it being of Earth, because Earth that is too cold does not strengthen or produce Earth.

The Chinese classics do state one benefit of Yang Metal being born during winter, which is that the state of Metal is purer. So, if the required elements do appear in the natal chart and allow Yang Metal to be forged, the chart-holder is often considered very elegant. He may have an aura of grace surrounding him. Such charts are extremely rare, however.

YANG METAL WINTER 2021: As Metal is considered weak in winter months, some Fire will be required to strengthen Earth and get rid of the coldness of winter so that Yang Metal can become strong and get itself ready to be forged. The 2021 elements do not provide the critical ones required for a winter Yang Metal's quality to be uplifted. You might find yourself getting a bit too comfortable in 2021 as Fire isn't present, but know that this is just a phase. Instead of getting complacent, spend this time planning for the future.

Yin Metal (辛金)

Yin Metal's nature is soft. It is the kind of metal used to make ornaments and jewelry, as it is malleable. The elements required to bring out the best in Yin Metal are different when compared to Yang Metal, even though they are both Metal. Fire brings out the best in Yang Metal, but it is Water that brings out the best in Yin Metal, so we can't assume that both types of Metal will have the same requirements.

SPRING

February to April
(寅, 卯, 辰). Yin / Mao / Chen. 1st to 3rd Solar Months.

Similar to Yang Metal, Yin Metal is at its weakest during spring and is not in a state to be cleansed and have its value extracted. Your Year Branch of *Chou* here will be extremely beneficial for Yin Metal, as the growth and strengthening of Yin Metal take priority. If they don't, there will be nothing to cleanse in the first place.

The Wood of spring ensures that an influx of wealth will always be there for you, but the bigger question is whether your Yin Metal Daymaster is strong enough to take on the strong presence of Wood. When Yin Metal is too weak for Wood, it breaks, so its presence does not actually translate into the ability to acquire wealth, but rather a burden caused by wealth. You'll likely find yourself having to chase after a paycheck if Wood overpowers Metal because it is considered a taboo for the element representing wealth to overpower the Daymaster. If Yin Metal gets enough support from other areas of your natal chart or your Elemental Phase—and on top of that, if Water appears as well—wealth will definitely be in abundance, and it will likely come to you easily.

That being said, take note if Yin Metal's strength becomes excessive, especially when the source of strength comes from the Earth element. This indicates that you are getting too comfortable and sheltered, which, generally speaking, translates into a lack of progress in life. Yin Metal is particularly sensitive to the Earth element, as Earth has the ability to rapidly bring down Yin Metal's quality. As such, whether your Year Branch plays a positive or negative role in a chart like yours really depends on the elements appearing in other parts of your natal chart. If your Yin Metal is already in a strong state, the Year Branch will manifest as a challenging family environment and also a lack of affinity with positive role models and superiors, which will naturally get in the way of your progress.

YIN METAL SPRING 2021: As a spring Yin Metal is likely weak, 2021's elements will be supportive, so expect 2021 to be a year when you get to experience some financial and career progress. However, if excessive Earth and Metal appear in other parts of your chart, the opposite will be true, and you will feel pressure instead of growth. Losing your source of wealth and income is likely.

SUMMER

May to July
(巳, 午, 未) Si / Wu / Wei. 4th to 6th Solar Months.

As someone under the Ox zodiac, your Year Branch is of Wet Earth. Your Month Branch is Fire during summer, or Earth if you were born during the sixth solar month (July). Earth's presence here is also strengthened by the Fire of summer. Neither Earth nor Fire are elements that are known to bring out the best in Yin Metal, and Yin Metal in such a state desperately requires some remedying. Such a chart would need Water first and foremost, not just to save Yin Metal from being melted by summer's Fire, but also to cleanse Yin Metal from the possible excessive Earth in the chart, especially if you were born during the sixth solar month of *Wei* (July).

Your natal chart quality will be very dependent on whether Water appears in other parts of your natal chart. As Water represents the Output God, when the Water element appears in a chart like this, the chart-holder will naturally be imbued with artistic talents and have a gift for communication. But take note that the Water elements here must not be harmed by or clash with Earth as that will impede these natural talents.

YIN METAL SUMMER 2021: For chart-holders born during the fourth and fifth solar months (May and June), 2021 will feel more like a neutral year because Wet Earth protects Yin Metal from summer's Fire, but significant progress is unlikely. For people born during the sixth solar month, if Water does not appear but additional Earth or Fire does, success in general will be much harder to achieve, and the chart-holder will lack the elegance and ability to influence others, which Yin Metal is known for.

AUTUMN

August to October
(申, 酉, 戌) Shen / You / Xu. 7th to 9th Solar Months.

Yin Metal is definitely strong during autumn and even more so as your Year Branch is an Earth Branch. Yin Metal is getting a lot of support in your chart, and it is ready to be cleansed and have its value extracted.

From a technical perspective, it is unlikely that your Year Branch and Month Branch act as supporting elements in your chart, which means that your success has to come from your own efforts and talents, as it is very unlikely that you were born into a supportive environment in which a lot of financial and emotional support were available to you. The appearance of the Water element in your natal chart as well as Elemental Phases is important for such charts, because the Output Gods, which Water manifests as, are the ones that generally determine whether the chart-holder is imbued with a special talent. If Wood also happens to appear at the same time, then these talents will be translated into the ability to acquire wealth as well.

YIN METAL AUTUMN 2021: Additional Earth elements should not appear, as they play no constructive role in uplifting the quality of your chart. Earth's presence does act as a pollutant to Water and inhibits Water's ability to cleanse Yin Water and inhibits the growth of the chart-holder. As such, 2021 will not be a beneficial year for Yin Metal chart-holders born during autumn, and it is likely that financial stresses will manifest because Wood, representing wealth, is harmed by Metal.

WINTER

November to January
(亥, 子, 丑) Hai / Zi / Chou. 10th to 12th Solar Months.

Your Year Branch is Earth and your Month Branch is Water. In this case, the support from Earth prepares Yin Earth for cleansing. The nature of Yin Metal is such that Water brings out the best in it, so when Yin Metal is in a strong state, instead of using Fire to forge it the way we do for Yang Metal, we want Water to cleanse it instead. Yin Metal is already malleable, so Fire is unnecessary in this case and not an ideal element to use.

The appearance of both Earth and Water in this chart can be seen as a good thing, as this combination supports Yin Metal's growth and cleansing. The inclusion of Wood can improve this chart even more. Wood's presence ensures that the cleansing of Yin Metal is thorough, because although Earth can give birth to Yin Metal, too much Earth can pollute or stain Yin Metal. As with all other charts, the key to the quality of a chart like this is to ensure all these interplaying elements are balanced and don't overpower each other.

From the perspective of a Yin Metal person, too much Earth leads to being too sheltered and lethargic; too much Water leads to overextending oneself and overestimating one's abilities. Too much Wood breaks Yin Metal, leading to the chart-holder feeling overwhelmed and not able to achieve more. In summary, as a Yin Metal person born during winter, you must first have Earth come into the picture to strengthen Yin Metal and then introduce other elements like Water and Wood to ensure Earth does not end up burying Yin Metal instead.

It'll be difficult to deduce the role your Year Branch and Month Branch will play without looking at other parts of the chart, so the manifestations of each may play out in a number of ways. If your chart ends up being a balanced one, the strong presence of Water during winter will bless you with abundance. If your Yin Metal chart happens to be in a balanced state, communication and the ability to influence will also come naturally for you, as Water represents your Output Gods, and you might even have an artistic flair.

YIN METAL WINTER 2021: If your chart has additional Water or Wood, then 2021 will be a positive year for you because the additional Earth and Metal from 2021 will strengthen and balance your Yin Metal Daymaster. Progress, especially financially, is very likely. However, if your Day and Hour Pillars have additional Earth and Metal, then these elements will be in excess, which means 2021's elements will start to have a detrimental effect on you; so expect increased competition and don't take on more than you can handle—but the potentially negative effects for Yin Metal chart-holders born in winter will not be as severe as they will be for Yin Metal people born during autumn.

Yang Water (壬水)

Yang Water is fast, uncontrollable moving torrents symbolized by rapid streams and waterfalls. It is not the kind of water that can be harnessed by humans. Yang Water is best used for cleansing and removing impurities as well as cooling down hot, arid environments.

SPRING

February to April
(寅, 卯, 辰). Yin / Mao / Chen. 1st to 3rd Solar Months.

Yang Water during spring is usually considered weak, but the presence of your Year Branch of *Chou* does provide some form of support. The Year Branch of *Chou* plays a positive role in your chart, so your family's influence on you will be a positive one. A family member may play an active role as your partner, mentor, or disciplinarian as the *Chou* Branch holds three different kinds of elements, all of which have their own positive, unique influence on Yang Water.

YANG WATER SPRING 2021: 2021's elements will have a positive effect for a springtime Yang Water chart-holder, as the Metal that appears helps control Wood and strengthen Water. It will be a good year to further studies and artistic pursuits as the Metal from 2021 represents the Resource God, which holds dominion over scholastic pursuits.

SUMMER

May to July
(巳, 午, 未) Si / Wu / Wei. 4th to 6th Solar Months.

Despite having a clashing relationship, Water and Fire share a special bond in which each element's best side cannot be brought out without the presence of the other. Water makes sure Fire does not emerge uncontrollably, whereas Fire makes sure Water is warm enough to nourish life. Fire and Water must be in a balanced state and be of equal strength for this to happen.

For a Yang Water person born during summer, Fire definitely overpowers Water, so such charts will need the Daymaster to become strong through the presence of additional Metal and Water, enhancing a chart-holder's ability to acquire wealth smoothly, as Fire represents Water's wealth.

Your Year Branch will play a meaningful role in making sure Yang Water gets some support, as *Chou* does hold some Water and Metal and helps make sure your chart does not end up becoming too arid from summer.

If you were born during the sixth solar month of *Wei* (July), there will be a clash between your Year Branch and Month Branch, and this clash strengthens Earth, which is detrimental to your Yang Water Daymaster. This clash affects your beneficial elements, and as the elements represent your mother especially, this may manifest as her having a difficult time in general. Your relationship with her may suffer as well. Encountering additional Metal is extremely important for charts like these.

YANG WATER SUMMER 2021: 2021 can be considered a supportive year for people born during the fourth or fifth solar months (May or June), especially if additional Water exists in the natal chart. For people born during the sixth solar month (July), there is too much Earth in the chart. This excess has to be balanced out with additional Wood in the chart; if not, a difficult year is very likely, and negative change will be forced upon you due to multiple clashes appearing between the *Chou* and *Wei* Branches.

AUTUMN

August to October
(申, 酉, 戌) Shen / You / Xu. 7th to 9th Solar Months.

Yang Water during autumn starts to gain some strength, so the role of your Ox Year Branch begins to become ambiguous. It's important to avoid your chart becoming imbalanced due to Yang Water becoming too strong.

For people born during the seventh or eighth solar months of *Shen* (August) and *You* (September): Should you find that additional Water and Metal appears in your Day and Hour Pillars, you'll likely be a bit too introverted or repressed for your own good, being extremely risk averse and not wanting to be in the limelight. Academic achievements will be limited as well, and your overall progress may be stifled, so watch out for these tendencies. To address this from a theoretical perspective, your chart will welcome Wood and Fire. Wood, in this case, would be your Output God, which helps with expression and the process of putting your thoughts into action, whereas Fire represents your ability and resourcefulness at acquiring wealth.

For people born during the ninth solar month of *Xu* (October), you'll need to constantly watch your relationship with superiors and people in positions of authority, as a *Chou-Xu* punishment Branch interaction appears. Finding benefactors older than you who can give you the right opportunities will be particularly difficult, so it's important for you to make it a point to become a person who can attract mentors who are inclined to help you.

YANG WATER AUTUMN 2021: People born during the ninth solar month of *Xu* (October) need to pay special attention to the year 2021, because an Earth combination formed by *Chou*, *Wei,* and *Xu* creates excessive strengthening of Earth and is extremely harmful to Yang Water. It is commonly known as the bullying punishment which will do what its name suggests, so you'll find yourself having a lot of people problems to deal with, although it is not your fault and just reflects a harsh environment.

WINTER

November to January
(亥, 子, 丑) Hai / Zi / Chou. 10th to 12th Solar Months.

Yang Water is at its strongest during winter, and it can become destructive. Yang Water resembles strong, rapid bodies of water that are not easily controlled. Although your Year Branch is an Earth Branch, do remember that *Chou* is of Wet Earth, and it does not do a good job of containing Water, let alone controlling it. On top of that, the existence of *Chou* also means Water combinations may form, allowing Water's strength to be even more dominant.

If additional Water or Metal exists in your chart, you'll need to work on calming your mind. Negative thoughts will likely flood your mind on a constant basis, so you'll need to figure out how to clear it when that happens. Water represents intellect and cognitive abilities in metaphysics, but an imbalance will cause the chart-holder's mind to venture to places it does not need to be.

A chart in this state will require the appearance of Dry Earth or Yang Earth to keep Yang Water in check, and ideally Fire is present to help strengthen Earth as well. Yang Earth is the form of Earth that is strong enough to hold Yang Water, and you could see Yang Earth as controlling the chart-holder's mind, giving him or her more structure and mental calmness.

YANG WATER WINTER 2021: The 2021 year's Metal and Wet Earth elements do not help to remedy the flaws of a winter-born Yang Water chart, so it's unlikely 2021 will be considered a beneficial year unless Wood and Fire elements appear in other areas of your natal chart or Elemental Phases. Academic pursuits will likely not go well, and financial stress will arise too.

Yin Water (癸水)

As the gentler version of Water, Yin Water is one that can truly provide nourishment. Symbolizing rain, the morning dew, and the water we use in day-to-day life, Yin Water's value comes from remaining pure so that it can be used by humans. The element that is its greatest antagonist is Earth, as Earth pollutes Water. Although Earth represents the Officer God for Water, which represents title and leadership, its effects will not manifest in Yin Water's case because of this relationship.

SPRING

February to April
(寅, 卯, 辰). Yin / Mao / Chen. 1st to 3rd Solar Months.

Yin Water during spring is at its purest, because Wood has a purifying effect on Water. However, before purification can be done, Yin Water needs to be strong enough for its intrinsic value to show. As your Year Branch is of Earth, having Wood in your Month Branch can be a good thing. However, your Yin Water Daymaster must have enough support from other parts of the natal chart, or at least your Elemental Phases. Should your Yin Water Daymaster be in a strong enough state, the presence of Wood will be beneficial for you and imbue you with creative abilities, as well as bring out the nurturing side of Yin Water.

For people born during the third solar month of *Chen* (April), Earth starts to get a bit excessive, as both your Year Branch and Month Branch will be Earth, so you'll definitely need Wood to appear somewhere else in your chart for Yin Water to be purified. If Yin Water in such a state is not purified, the nurturing side of Yin Water will not manifest, and the chart-holder loses his or her ability to influence others. The Officer God starts to play a negative role in the chart, and it will manifest as a tendency to get into trouble with authority instead. As Water also represents intelligence under the Five Commons, excessive Earth also hinders the Yin Water chart-holder from being able to think clearly, apply practical wisdom, and make better decisions for themselves.

YIN WATER 2021: The priority for Yin Water charts will be strength in order to achieve artistic and creative goals. 2021's Yin Metal will definitely help, although with a caveat—Yin Water's most disliked element, which is Earth, appears, so expect some obstacles to get in the way of your goals.

SUMMER

May to July
(巳, 午, 未) Si / Wu / Wei. 4th to 6th Solar Months.

It's often argued that Yin Water is at its best during summer. Yin Water becomes purified during spring, and summer is the period where Yin Water is put in a state in which it can truly be put to use, as the bitter cold is removed from Water, allowing Yin Water to truly act as a nourisher of life. However, as with all charts, everything must be balanced, and Yin Water cannot be too weak.

If you are a Yin Water chart-holder born during the fourth solar month of *Si* (May) or fifth solar month of *Wu* (June), your Yin Water is very likely weak and you will require Water and Metal to appear in other parts of your chart for Yin Water's best qualities, such as clear-thinking and wisdom, to manifest. 2021's Yin Metal and Wet Earth will help you achieve this, but take note that you will need to have additional Metal or Water elements in your chart.

If you happen to be born in the sixth solar month of *Wei* (July), the issue of having too much Earth will arise again, due to the clash between the two Earth Branches of *Chou* and *Wei*. You will need Wood's presence when this occurs to keep Yin Water pure. In the absence of Wood, a chart where *Chou* and *Wei* clash will likely manifest as a hostile family environment in which the chart-holder's parents don't have the best relationship. This is due to the fact that the elements representing the mother and father are both harmed as a result of the clash between *Chou* and *Wei*. The year 2021 will not be a beneficial one for such charts, as Earth becomes excessive.

YIN WATER SUMMER'S 2021: People born during the fourth or fifth solar months (May or June) will likely benefit from 2021's elements. As Yin Metal here shows up as the Indirect Resource God, picking up knowledge or skills, especially in an esoteric or less popular field, will be very beneficial. People in research should also expect a good year due to Indirect Resource showing up. If you were born during the sixth solar month (July), which has Earth, you may require Wood to appear instead. Clear thinking is impeded, so make sure you think through your decisions carefully.

AUTUMN

August to October
(申, 酉, 戌) Shen / You / Xu. 7th to 9th Solar Months.

Yin Water is strong during autumn and will start to exhibit the same qualities as Yang Water, so what it needs won't be too different. The Metal of autumn significantly strengthens Yin Water, and the Year Branch that is of Wet Earth also supports Yin Water. Encountering Fire and Wood would be critical for a chart like yours, as Yin Water needs to undergo a bit of processing for its value to manifest. Wood ensures that Yin Water remains pure and also acts as the source of Fire's strength, whereas Fire ensures that Water does not become too cold to be used. High quality, autumn-born Yin Water charts will always have Wood and Fire present.

Similar to Yang Water, Yin Water people born during the seventh and eighth solar months (July and August) will need to ensure that their Daymasters do not end up becoming too strong with additional Water or Metal appearing elsewhere, as this combination will likely manifest as mental and emotional struggle for the chart-holder. This is where Wood and Fire come in, as they prevent Yin Water from over-strengthening. People born during the ninth solar month (September) will need to watch for the *Chou-Xu* punishment Branch interaction in 2021, which strengthens Earth and pollutes Yin Water, resulting in implications for one's career advancement and relationship with superiors. If you have an excessively strong Water chart, regardless of whether you are Yang or Yin Water, you may be led to overthinking and pessimism, because Water's overabundance will negatively impact your mood, so watch out for excessive Water elements appearing in your chart.

YIN WATER AUTUMN 2021: Yin Water is purest during autumn, and we generally want to avoid Earth in such charts. For Yin Metal people born during autumn, 2021 will be laden with obstacles due to Earth appearing. Yin Metal also harms Wood, which is a critical element for Yin Water. Do not rush any important decisions this year, as you might not be able to see the full picture. As Wood represents creativity and communication, extra effort in these aspects will help you achieve your goals, so don't be afraid to talk to others and bounce ideas off of them.

WINTER

November to January
(亥, 子, 丑) Hai / Zi / Chou. 10th to 12th Solar Months.

Any Yin polarity that becomes too strong will start to exhibit Yang polarity traits. As such, Yin Water starts to exhibit traits of Yang Water during winter as Water becomes too strong and the calm, stagnant nature of Yin Water starts to change. Similar to an overly strong Yang Water chart, Yin Water in such a state is destructive, so control has to be exerted in the form of Yang Earth, with Fire coming in to support Earth's strength. The Year Branch of *Chou* does not play a meaningful role in the chart and poses a risk of a Water combination forming as well, so it is unlikely a chart like this will have the family members playing a supportive role in the chart-holder's life. Success will have to come purely from the chart-holder's effort and volition.

YIN WATER WINTER 2021: Generally speaking, 2021 won't give these chart-holders a lift, elements-wise, as a strong Yang Water chart will no longer need Metal, and the Wet Earth Branch of *Chou* is not an effective remedy for this chart's flaws. Maintaining stability and calmness of mind will be especially important in 2021. If you find additional Water or Metal elements in your natal chart, refrain from rushing important decisions and also keep active to regulate your mood better.

An End Note

Everything mentioned in this book is just the tip of the iceberg and merely introduces some core concepts that will help you explore this field with a bit more ease.

I was a skeptic myself before life pushed me in the direction of becoming a practitioner, but as I went deeper into the field, I couldn't help but be in awe of what the sages left us. Chinese astrology—astrology as a whole—has opened my eyes to a whole new way of seeing the world, the laws that govern it, and how our lives are a constant unfolding of its mysteries.

No words are enough to express how amazing our ancestors were, and I'm not just referring to my Chinese ancestors, but every sage from every civilization who looked to the stars and, through thousands of years of observation and tenacity, found meaning in them to guide us in leading better, more fulfilled lives.

I hope this book lights a fire in you to find out more, not just about the application of Chinese astrology, but also about the history, philosophy, and wisdom it has to offer—because that is where the real value lies.

Glossary

AUXILIARY STARS: The placement of these stars can be either auspicious or inauspicious, depending upon how they appear in your chart. They add a second layer of analysis to your forecast and how the events of your life might manifest.

BALANCED BAZI CHART: A term used to indicate a high-quality natal chart, which usually manifests as a more stable life with fewer obstacles.

BAZI: Popularly known as the "Four Pillars of Destiny." A Chinese astrological system of divining an individual's future using the sexagenary cycle.

BENEFICIAL ELEMENTS: The elements a chart needs for it to be in a more balanced state. The strengthening of beneficial elements indicates progress and achievement in life.

DAYMASTER: The reference point within your natal chart that represents your true nature and the core of your being. The state of your Daymaster and what it needs to achieve balance are determined by the season in which you were born and the other elements expressed through Stems and Branches in your chart.

DESTRUCTIVE ELEMENTS: The elements that cause a chart to become even more imbalanced. The strengthening of destructive elements leads to obstacles and negative manifestations.

EARTHLY BRANCH RELATIONSHIPS: The relationship between the Twelve Earthly Branches and how the elements within them interact with one another.

ELEMENTAL PHASES: These describe how an individual's life may unfold. A natal chart is the basis for understanding that individual's Elemental Phases.

POLARIS STAR ASTROLOGY: Another ancient method of Chinese astrology that uses the Polaris star and Big Dipper as reference points.

SEXAGENARY CYCLE: A sixty-year cycle used to measure time in China. This is the basis for a Bazi chart.

TEN GODS: Term used specifically in the Bazi method of Chinese astrology. Used to describe the relationship between one's Daymaster and other elements.

TEN HEAVENLY STEMS: Chinese system of ordinals made up of the Five Elements and their Yin and Yang polarities. Also used for measuring time.

TWELVE EARTHLY BRANCHES: Chinese ordering system that was built from observations of the orbit of Jupiter. Used for measuring time.

TWELVE ZODIAC SIGNS: The lay term for the Twelve Earthly Branches. Both refer to the same system of timekeeping.

YIN AND YANG: Concept of dualism in Chinese cosmology, with reality existing as opposing forces.

Acknowledgments

First and foremost, I would like to thank the editor and publisher for giving me this opportunity to write this book, giving me a louder voice to reach more people and educate them on the right ways to use astrology.

This is my first very book that I have never even dreamed of writing, and I hope it's the first of many to come. I'm incredibly grateful for this opportunity to share Chinese metaphysics and astrology with everyone.

I wish to thank the publishing team that made this possible, especially my editor, Kate Zimmermann, who is the living embodiment of what having a benefactor means. The lucky stars in my astrological chart would mean nothing if not for people like Kate. Thank you for your patience and guidance and for making this book possible.

Index

Note: Page numbers in **bold** indicate glossary definitions.

About the Author

An old soul trapped in a young man's body, Sean Chan is a self-taught practitioner and thought-leader in his field who found his affinity to Chinese metaphysics through the classical texts of feudal China.

One of the leading Chinese metaphysics practitioners in Southeast Asia, Sean serves a global clientele and dedicates himself to helping his clients lead better lives using Chinese astrology and feng shui. He addresses modern-day misconceptions and malpractices on his blog and hopes to restore Chinese metaphysics to its former glory, so that one day, everyone can benefit from it the way the Chinese sages intended. You can visit him online at www.masterseanchan.com or on Facebook (@masterSeanChan).